# 365 READING Activities

**Contributing Writers:**
Suzanne I. Barchers, Ed.D.
Marilee Robin Burton
Beth Alley Wise

**Consultant:**
Leslie Anne Perry, Ph.D.

**Illustrators:**
Kate Flanagan
Lynn Sweat

D1451412

**BACKPACKBOOKS**
○
**NEW YORK**

## Contributing Writers:

**Suzanne I. Barchers, Ed.D.,** has written numerous books and articles on reading, language arts, and literacy for children. She serves as an affiliate faculty member at the University of Colorado, Denver, and is a former educator, reading specialist, and administrator at public and private schools of Denver.

**Marilee Robin Burton** is a freelance educational writer, consultant, and language arts specialist. She has ten years of experience as a teacher and has contributed to several publications, including *Early Childhood Workshop* and *Literary Place.* She is also the author and artist for several children's picture books and has a master of arts degree in early childhood education and human development.

**Beth Alley Wise** is an early childhood education specialist and the author of over 50 children's books, including *Beginning to Read, Key Words to Reading,* and *My Reading Kit.* She has written and edited textbooks and software for numerous educational publishers and serves as a developmental specialist on reading reforms.

## Consultant:

**Leslie Anne Perry, Ph.D.** is Assistant Professor for the Department of Curriculum and Instruction at East Tennessee State University. She has a Ph.D. in elementary education with a specialization in reading and a master of sciences degree in early childhood education. She has contributed to several books on reading for educators, and her articles have appeared in several educational publications, including *Educational Oasis, Teaching K–8* and *Illinois Reading Council Journal.*

Additional consultation was provided by Elizabeth Crosby Stull, Ph.D., Assistant Professor of Language and Literacy, Childrens' Literature, Ohio State University. She has written several books, including curriculum activity guides for The Center for Applied Research in Education, and is a member of the International Reading Association and the National Association for Education of Young Children.

**Illustrators:** Kate Flanagan, Lynn Sweat
**Front and Back Cover Illustrations:** Anne Kennedy

Copyright © 2004 by Publications International, Ltd.

This 2004 edition published by Backpack Books, by arrangement with Publications International, Ltd.

Backpack Books
122 Fifth Ave.
New York, NY 10011

ISBN 0-7607-5254-0

Printed and bound in China.

04 05 06 07 08 MCH 10 9 8 7 6 5 4 3 2 1

# Contents

# INTRODUCTION

*365 Reading Activities* might lead one to believe that this book is restricted to the activity of reading. In reality, this book contains an appealing array of exciting, motivating, and educational language arts activities, all of which contribute to your child's reading development.

Reading, writing, listening, and speaking are the four major areas of language arts. Each of these language forms reinforces the other. Therefore, activities that focus on writing,

listening, and speaking develop and reinforce skills necessary for reading success. From creating picture dictionaries and word webs to inventive storytelling and creative writing, your child will gain a better understanding of the elements needed to become a more confident reader.

When guiding your child through these activities, the goal should always be to provide a positive learning experience. Take the time to go over the instructions carefully with your child, have patience, and use praise and encouragement. Each activity has been rated with a difficulty level: *easy, medium,* or *challenging.* Book symbols near the title of each activity represent the degree of difficulty: Three books indicate activities that are challenging, two books indicate activities that require intermediate skills, and one book indicates activities that are easy. And even though the activities are labeled by their level of difficulty, *all* activities are on the same level of fun. These designations are here to provide guidance as you select activities for your child. Remember, though, that children learn at

activities designed to enhance a particular skill. The first four chapters relate specifically to reading, followed by three chapters related to writing, two chapters that cover listening and speaking, and one chapter that focuses on developing thinking skills.

Chapter 1 (Literature Links) is designed to get the child started on a lifetime of pleasure with books. Through the activities in this chapter, your child will develop the habit of reading. After all, reading is the key that opens the door to a whole world of information.

Reading without comprehension or understanding, however, is not actual reading. Chapter 2 (Comprehension Capers) offers an exciting array of activities designed to generate enthusiasm for reading while building skills necessary for comprehension.

different rates. An activity that may be easy for one child may be challenging for another child of the same age. Therefore, regardless of the age of your child, you may want to start with some of the activities designated as *easy* and work up. All of the activities in this book can be enhanced through interaction with an adult. However, some of the activities require close adult supervision for safety reasons, such as activities that require the use of scissors or other implements; some even involve cooking. Be sure to read all the instructions carefully and adhere to any words of caution.

This book is divided into ten chapters. Each chapter focuses on a different element of reading and contains a wide variety of

Written passages that a child reads are made up of individual words. Your child can read with comprehension only if the meaning of these words are recognized and understood. The activities in Chapter 3 (Word Quests) engages your child in lively word play while improving basic vocabulary skills.

Chapter 4 (Phonics Fortunes) delves into reinforcing word recognition skills, which allow the child to read more independently. Creative activities such as Letter Collage and Simon Says offer inventive and fun ways for the child to learn letter sounds. And learning to apply phonics skills to unknown words will help the child comprehend what is being read.

Chapter 5 (Writing Roundups), the first of the writing chapters, presents

activities that strengthen and reinforce reading skills through poems, songs, and other writing exercises. Reading and writing are simply two heads of the same coin. The child who is a competent writer usually excels at reading and vice versa.

Spelling is one of the tools that makes written communication possible. Chapter 6 (Spelling Specials) offers an inventive selection of spelling escapades, which guarantee to reinforce your child's spelling skills. Spelling and phonics are also closely related. The child who learns to attend to the sounds represented by letters while learning to spell words, can use this knowledge of letter/sound relationships when he or she decodes unknown words encountered while reading.

Grammar is another tool that enhances written communication. Chapter 7 (Grammar

Grabbers) focuses on appealing activities that help the young reader develop knowledge about parts of speech and other elements of grammar, such as the use of nouns, verbs, and adjectives.

Listening is the first communication skill that the child utilizes. Chapter 8 (Listening Launches) invites the young learner to enhance good listening skills through this selection of contagious listening activities.

Speaking, an integral part of oral language development, is also closely related to reading development. Chapter 9 (Speaking Sparks) utilizes activities that help develop speaking skills, for it is much easier for the child to learn to read words already used verbally.

The final chapter, Chapter 10 (Using Brain Power), helps develop the child's thinking skills. Cognitive processing (thinking) is central to all four of the language arts. And the development of critical thinking skills is essential for reading success.

The activities within the various chapters are not in any particular order, so feel free to skip around throughout the book. Your child may respond well to a particular type of activity. For example, if your child likes to look at pictures in magazines, you may want to follow up on another day with a picture activity. Just look for one in the index. The new activity could be from the same chapter or from a different chapter. In order to keep track of the activities you and your child have done, you may want to use a pencil to make a check mark beside each activity as it is completed.

In conclusion, it is the sincere hope of the authors and editors of *365 Reading Activities* that the ideas set forth in this book will be helpful to you as you work with your child during these very special years. You play a critical role in your child's reading development—you are your child's first teacher. With your guidance, your child can grow in both competence and confidence as he or she embarks on one of life's most wondrous and rewarding adventures—reading!

# LITERATURE LINKS

Children who are read to at home actually do better in reading at school. In addition, the child is exposed to new vocabulary words and how they sound. The child also gains familiarity with books and learns that print is read from left to right. The following activities in this chapter range from dressing up as a favorite character to eating through the alphabet. Some require a trip to the library; others require only a trip to your bookshelf. Many of the books will inspire you to create your own reading activities.

## ALPHABET EATING

*Learn new words and try new foods while you create a menu for many meals to come.*

**WHAT YOU'LL NEED:** alphabet book that deals with food

Read the alphabet book together. Then read the book again, but this time have the child point to and read the words. Next list all the foods illustrated and organize them from A to Z. Some letters will have more than one food, other letters will have none, but include all of them.

Now plan what foods to eat over the course of a week, with the intention of eating through the alphabet. Use the letters with several choices to provide a series of menus that are balanced and interesting. Write up a menu for each meal and have the child read the food words. At the end of the week evaluate the process. Was it fun? Did the child learn some new words and try some new foods?

# POETRY FUN

*Inspire the young reader by exploring humorous*
*poetry and having fun at the same time.*

**WHAT YOU'LL NEED:** collection of humorous poems

Read a number of funny poems together. Invite the child to predict the words that will rhyme or the words that will complete the lines. Discuss which rhymes are the funniest. Then have the child choose one poem and practice reading it aloud, adding gestures and voices when appropriate. Encourage the child to make the gestures as funny as possible.

# PICTURE READING

**3**

*This activity is sure to help a beginning reader*
*get excited about reading.*

**WHAT YOU'LL NEED:** any illustrated book that has a few simple words on each page, sticky notes

Choose a book that has words the child uses when talking or playing. For example, a book on toys or animals would be good. Each page should have just one or two words. Cover one of the words with a sticky note. Have the child describe the illustration. Then remove the sticky note and compare the illustration to the text. If the child identified a word that was a good choice but different, discuss how sometimes different words can be part of the same idea expressed in the illustration.

# BAD DAY, BETTER DAY

**4**

*Reading this book combined with a little discussion can turn a bad day into a better day.*

**WHAT YOU'LL NEED:** *Alexander and the Terrible, Horrible, No Good, Very Bad Day* by Judith Viorst, paper, pencil

Read the story aloud with the child when he or she is having a bad day. Then make a list of all the things that were terrible in the story. Next discuss all the events that happened to the child during the day, and make another list comprised of those events. Compare the two lists. Then discuss ways to make a bad day better. List these, also.

**5**

# BOOKS OF A FEATHER

*Compare two books from the same genre to see why they are favorites.*

**WHAT YOU'LL NEED:** two favorite books from the same genre, such as fairy tales, fantasies, biographies, etc.

Encourage the child to read or reread both books. Then have the child make a list of the characteristics in each book. Discuss with the child how the characteristics are alike. How are they different? Which book did the child like better? Are the characters in each book similar? Do the books have similar story lines?

## 6 CLIFF-HANGERS

*The child will enjoy reading a good cliff-hanger while practicing reading and comprehension skills.*

**WHAT YOU'LL NEED:** *Charlotte's Web* or *The Trumpet of the Swan* by E. B. White, tape recorder

Read one of the above "cliff-hanger" stories into a tape recorder. Then have the child read the book while listening to the tape. This will help the child read and understand the text. After each chapter, stop the tape recorder and invite the child to predict what will happen next. Discuss the prediction together. Then have the child read the next chapter to find out if the prediction is correct. Continue the activity until the book is finished.

## CREATING A CHARACTER 7

*An imaginative child will enjoy becoming a favorite character for a day!*

**WHAT YOU'LL NEED:** favorite book or story

Invite the child to choose a favorite character from a favorite book. Help the child find descriptive passages that tell about the character. Then invite the child to decide how the character would dress and act. For example, a very old lady might wear a shawl, use a handbag, and walk hunched over while using a cane. Have a dress-up day when the child dresses up as the character and reads aloud portions of the book.

# 8 MATCH THAT PICTURE!

*In this activity, the beginning reader will practice comprehension while matching words with pictures.*

**WHAT YOU'LL NEED:** any picture book with many illustrations of objects in it

Before reading the book aloud, look at all the illustrations and discuss them with the child. Invite the child to point to and name interesting objects in the illustrations.

Then read the story aloud to the child while he or she looks on. Have the child find words in the text that match the objects in the illustrations. If there are illustrations without matching words, list the words on a piece of paper and discuss their meaning.

## ACTIVITY TWIST

To encourage creative thinking, read a story with no pictures. Then help the child determine what illustrations might be used in the story.

# SHARED READING

**9**

*One of the best memories you can give a child is sharing a favorite book together.*

**WHAT YOU'LL NEED:** favorite book that is comfortable for the child to read aloud

Begin by reading aloud the first page of the book. Then have the child read the second page. Continue taking turns until the entire book is read. If the book is long, take turns reading paragraphs or half pages. Make the reading fun, and help the child with any unknown words when necessary.

**10**

# LET'S TELL A STORY!

*Encourage the young storyteller to share a favorite story.*

**WHAT YOU'LL NEED:** any favorite fairy tale

Invite the child to choose a favorite fairy tale that he or she would like to read to an audience. Encourage the child to read it aloud several times to you. Then have the child tell the story in his or her own words without thinking about the author's exact words. Discuss gestures that would add interest to the telling and would help the listeners understand the story, such as waving a magic wand or sprinkling fairy dust. Finally encourage the child to rehearse in front of a mirror before sharing the story with an audience.

# NEW ENDINGS

▼▼▼▼▼▼▼▼▼▼▼▼▼▼▼▼▼▼▼▼▼▼▼▼▼▼▼▼▼▼▼▼

*The child will learn how to write new story endings after reading this popular book.*

**WHAT YOU'LL NEED:** *Jumanji* by Chris Van Allsburg, paper, pencil

In this book, Peter and Judy find a game called "Jumanji, A Jungle Adventure Game." While playing the game, it comes to life and they must carefully follow the rules to escape life-threatening situations. When Peter and Judy are finished, they return the game to a park where the Budwing children, known for never following instructions, pick up the game.

Begin by reading the book together. Discuss what might happen if the Budwing children play the game by following the rules. Then write the Budwing's story together to share with others.

# SPORTS HEROES

■ ■ ■ ■ ■ ■ ■ ■ ■ ■ ■ ■ ■ ■ ■ ■ ■ ■

*This creative reading and recording activity is for sports fans of all ages.*

**WHAT YOU'LL NEED:** book about a favorite sports figure, newspapers or magazines with information about the person, notebook, pencil

Read through a book about a favorite sports figure together. Then scan the newspapers or magazines for additional information about the person. Invite the child to start a notebook that records facts or statistics about the sports figure. Add to it regularly.

# REPEATING READING

**13**

*Reading repeated lines is fun, especially in this beautiful story of life in the mountains.*

**WHAT YOU'LL NEED:** *When I Was Young in the Mountains* by Cynthia Rylant with illustrations by Diane Goode

Read the story aloud to the child and talk about the pictures. Read the story again and have the child read each repeated line. For additional discussion, share similar memories with the child.

**14**

# WILD THINGS

*Use this favorite story and activity when a child is feeing particularly wild!*

**WHAT YOU'LL NEED:** *Where the Wild Things Are* by Maurice Sendak, shoe box, clay, miscellaneous craft materials (colored paper, paints, etc.)

Read the book aloud and discuss the illustrations together. Use the illustrations of the land of the wild things to inspire a diorama, which is a three dimensional representation of a scene. Next make a diorama together.

Begin by inviting the child to paint one long side of the inside of the box green. This will be the ground when the box is turned on its side. Then paint the remaining sides blue for the sky. Trees can be added with paint if desired. To construct the inside, turn the shoe box on its side with the green side on the bottom. Then invite the child to use various craft materials to create grass, trees, and so on. Use the clay to fashion the wild things, Max, and any other features desired. Display the diorama next to the book. Then use the diorama when retelling or rereading the story.

**15**

# CATERPILLAR MENU

*This delicious activity just may become a favorite for the child.*

**WHAT YOU'LL NEED:** *The Very Hungry Caterpillar* by Eric Carle, 3×5 index cards, markers, paper

Begin by writing all the food words found in the book on the index cards. Then read the book together. Next match the words on the cards to the pages they appear on in the book. Invite the child to arrange the words in the same order they are found in the book. Then create a menu for the caterpillar together, listing all the foods it ate.

# CURTAIN'S UP!

**16**

*These ideas will encourage the child to act out a favorite story.*

**WHAT YOU'LL NEED:** favorite picture book, paper, pencil

Read the book aloud together. Discuss with the child how to turn the book into a play. What parts will be the dialogue? What can be read aloud by a narrator? Help the child write a section of the book in script form. Then choose characters and read the script aloud together. To extend the activity, read the script into a tape recorder and share with others.

# READING WITH EXPRESSION

*Reading is always more fun when expression is added.*

**17**

**WHAT YOU'LL NEED:** any book that has strong rhythm or dialogue

Read the book aloud with the child. Try to read the story by using as much expression as possible, such as whispering, shouting, dragging out words, building up suspense, and so on. Depending on the text, dialogue, or events, invite the child to read the words in a loud, soft, fast, playful, or slow voice. For additional fun, have the child read the story into a tape recorder to share with others.

**18**

# FAIRY-TALE TURNAROUND

*This fairy-tale turnaround will inspire imaginative thinking in the young reader!*

**WHAT YOU'LL NEED:** favorite or familiar fairy tale

Read the fairy tale aloud together. Discuss its plot and then talk about what would happen if one of the bad characters was good. How would that affect the plot? What would happen to the other characters? How would the changed events affect the ending? Retell the story together with the new ending.

# TUESDAY'S TIME LINE

*Have you ever wondered what would happen if frogs could fly? Find out with this book.*

**WHAT YOU'LL NEED:** *Tuesday* by David Wiesner, paper, pencil

In this almost wordless book, frogs fly into town. Invite the child to tell the story from the illustrations. Then have the child list the events on paper, starting with the time the frogs arrived on Tuesday and ending with the time they leave. Help the child create a time line of the events.

## ACTIVITY TWIST

For an additional challenge, invite the child to write the words to the story or create a new story about pigs flying into town.

# 20 FUNNY SURPRISES

*Finding humor in illustrations is a great way
to add to the written story.*

**WHAT YOU'LL NEED:** *The Relatives Came* by Cynthia Rylant, with illustrations by Stephen Gammell

In this amusing story, a group of relatives show up for the summer. Read the book together. Then encourage the child to study the illustrations for amusing details, such as the car knocking down the fence or the dog eating part of the picnic. Talk about how the illustrator used humor to add to the written story. Discuss other books that use humor in illustrations as you come across them.

# DINOSAUR INFO 21

*This challenging, ongoing learning activity is a model
for increasing the child's knowledge base.*

**WHAT YOU'LL NEED:** 2 copies of dinosaur books

As scientists have made new discoveries, many older dinosaur books have become outdated. This gives you a good opportunity to show the child how learning never stops. Gather two books on dinosaurs from the library—one old and one new. Then search for some examples of facts that have changed with new information and discoveries. List those facts, then discuss them with the child. For an ongoing activity, invite the child to watch the newspapers and children's magazines at the library for more dinosaur information and use for later discussion.

# NURSERY RHYME INTERPLAY

**22**

*Familiar nursery rhymes can inspire endless story creations.*

**WHAT YOU'LL NEED:** favorite nursery rhymes

Read aloud several familiar nursery rhymes that the child knows and enjoys. Then invite the child to read the nursery rhymes aloud. Discuss what might happen if the characters met each other. For example, could Jack and Jill have saved Humpty Dumpty from falling off the wall? What would happen if the little old lady who lived in the shoe left her children with Peter Peter Pumpkin Eater? Have the child create new versions and share them with others.

**23**

# RHYMING GOOD TIME

*Reading words that rhyme is an easy and entertaining way to introduce new words to the young reader.*

**WHAT YOU'LL NEED:** any book that has rhyming text, such as ones by Dr. Seuss.

Read the rhymes aloud to the child, emphasizing the rhymes as they occur. Read the book again, but this time hesitate just before a rhyming word. Encourage the child to predict and point to the rhymes during the reading.

On another day, reread the story and encourage the child to identify even more portions of the text, especially entire lines that repeat rhymes. Remember to have the child point to at least some of the words while reading them aloud.

# 24 BIGRAPHY BOOK JACKET

*Writing words for a book jacket is a creative exercise that teaches the child summarization skills.*

**WHAT YOU'LL NEED:** biography or autobiography, paper, pencil

Explain to the child that a biography is a book written about someone's life and an autobiography is a book written by someone about his or her own life. Explain that a book jacket sometimes contains a summary of the book. For best results, look at other book jackets and see how the summaries were written. Then have the child read a biography or autobiography. After the child has finished, discuss the key events in the person's life. Invite the child to write a summary. Use the summary to create a book jacket for the biography or autobiography.

# PASTA MOSAIC 25

*You can never have too much pasta, right? Read what happens when a whole town gets too much!*

**WHAT YOU'LL NEED:** *Strega Nona* by Tomie dePaola, variety of dried pasta, glue, large square piece of cardboard or poster board, index cards

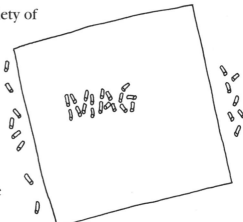

Read this story of a magic pasta pot and a young man who was disobedient. Choose a variety of important words from the story together, such as Anthony, magic, and Strega Nona, and write them on index cards. Use the pasta to create the words, using different colors or types to make the words interesting. Experiment with the placement of the pasta on the cardboard before gluing it into place. Use the cards to practice reading the words. Then reread the book.

# 26

# TALL TALES

*Everyone loves to exaggerate and embellish stories, especially when retelling tall tales.*

**WHAT YOU'LL NEED:** collection of tall tales, pencil, paper

Tall tales tell about American heroes who helped settle our country. They built the railroads, cleared the forests, and planted the apple trees. Some stories, such as Johnny Appleseed, have developed from the lives of real people.

Read a few tall tales to the child. Discuss all the exaggerations and embellishments in the tales. Can Pecos Bill's horse, Widow Maker, really bounce to the sky? What is real and what isn't? Discuss what makes these tales "tall," and list them on a piece of paper. For an additional challenge, try writing a tall tale together.

# COUNTING ALONG

# 27

*In this activity the child will combine counting with reading and writing.*

**WHAT YOU'LL NEED:** several counting books, paper, pencil, crayons or markers

Read and compare a variety of counting books together. Discuss what goes into a good counting book. Are accurate illustrations important? Does a story make the counting book more interesting? Plan to make a counting book. You may choose to make a book that goes from 1–20 or one that counts by 5's to 100. Then on each page of the new book, write the words and numerals. Invite the child to illustrate the book, too.

# THE MORAL OF THE STORY

▼▼▼▼▼▼▼▼▼▼▼▼▼▼▼▼▼▼▼▼▼▼▼▼▼▼▼▼▼

*What better way to teach a lesson than through a little story?*

**28**

**WHAT YOU'LL NEED:** collection of fables

Fables are short stories, usually involving animals, that teach lessons. Many are attributed to Aesop, the famous Greek writer of fables. Find one or more fables and take turns reading them. How many have people in them? Animals? What is the most common animal? For an additional challenge, make a list that keeps track of the number of foxes, crows, and other animals found in the fables. Then, most important, discuss what lessons are to be learned from each story.

**29**

# CREEPY CRAWLIES

━ ━ ━ ━ ━ ━ ━ ━ ━ ━ ━ ━ ━

*Using an interest in insects is a great way to inspire the reading of information books.*

**WHAT YOU'LL NEED:** any information book with photographs or drawings of spiders, ants, or other insects, notebook, pencil

Information books often have bright, colorful pictures, charts, and boxes containing special information. Choose a particular creepy crawly together, such as the ant, that is found in the book. Invite the child to read everything in the book about ants. Then look for ants outside together. Have the child make notes about the ants and compare the notes to the information found in the book. This process can be repeated several times during different seasons to see the changes that occur in the behavior of the chosen creepy crawly.

# FOLLOWING DIRECTIONS

*Here's an activity for the child to practice learning how to follow directions while being creative!*

**WHAT YOU'LL NEED:** simple craft book, various craft materials to complete chosen projects

Read the directions for a variety of craft projects together. Decide on one to make. Remember to explain to the child the importance of carefully following directions.

When finished, have the child reread the directions. Did the child follow them? If there were illustrations, did the child need to rely on them to understand the written directions? Try the same process with another project to reinforce the importance of following directions for craft projects.

# READING THE SIGNS

*Don't waste a minute of learning while running errands. Information is everywhere!*

Opportunities to read exist all around us. While running errands, going to school, or just walking around the neighborhood together, take notice of all the different signs. Then have the child read the signs with you. Discuss how the words start and end. Encourage the child to read them independently.

# AUTHOR! AUTHOR!

*The child will learn about an author while you help him or her do an author study.*

**WHAT YOU'LL NEED:** several books by a favorite author

Collect a variety of books by one author and read them with the child. This part may take several days. Then discuss the kind of writing the author does. Does the author retell folk tales, write about nature, or write fantasies? Then discuss the style of writing. Is the writing humorous, simple, or complex? Make a list of the author's characteristics.

## ACTIVITY TWIST

Vary this activity by using the same process for an illustrator study.

# THREE KIND MICE

33

*Become a new Mother Goose (or Father Gandor) while twisting old story lines into something new!*

**WHAT YOU'LL NEED:** nursery rhymes, paper, pencil

What if the mice were described as kind instead of blind? Maybe they wouldn't have had their tails cut off if they had been able to see. What if the old woman in the shoe bought a condo instead? Maybe her children would have behaved better with a nicer place to live.

Read a variety of rhymes together. Then help the child create new twists on the story line. Invite the child to make a small book of new nursery rhymes to share with others.

# 34 KEEPING A STORY IN ORDER

*Learn the importance of sequence in a story while documenting events through pictures and words.*

**WHAT YOU'LL NEED:** favorite book, large sheets of paper, pencil, markers or crayons

While the child reads the book, invite him or her to keep track of all the key events in the story, listing them in sequence. Help the child plan how to illustrate each of the major events in the story. Then on a large sheet of paper, draw enough boxes to hold all the events. Draw the boxes in rows from left to right. Number the boxes. Now invite the child to draw the events in the boxes, and write a short sentence that describes the event portrayed in each box. Then retell the story.

# 35 PREDICTION FUN

*This activity will engage the child in creative thinking while making predictions for an unfamiliar story.*

**WHAT YOU'LL NEED:** book that is unfamiliar to the child

Begin by reading the book and thinking about where the child can make predictions. Be sure that the illustrations do not give away the answers! Before you begin reading the book aloud to the child, plan to pause at certain points and ask the child to make a prediction. Accept all answers before continuing with the story. Be sure to enjoy any surprises and creativity the child displays when making predictions. Then invite the child to read the book for enjoyment.

# RADIO ADVERTISING 36

*Learn how to advertise a favorite book on the radio!*

**WHAT YOU'LL NEED:** favorite book, paper, pencil, tape recorder

Invite the child to reread a favorite book. Discuss what the child likes about the book and what makes it outstanding. Then help the child create an ad appropriate for reading on the radio. It should truly "sell" the book to listeners. Write down the ad. Then have the child practice reading it into a tape recorder until it is ready to be shared.

# WORD WALL

**37**

*Let words be a positive experience and a memory booster for the child with this creative activity.*

**WHAT YOU'LL NEED:** favorite books, large sheets of paper, markers

Hang several large sheets of paper on the wall. Place a variety of markers nearby. Explain that the child is going to fill the walls with words about books he or she has read, such as quotes, authors' names, titles, and so on. Remind the child how powerful punctuation can be. For example, if he or she really likes an author, the child might write the author's name, followed by an exclamation point.

**38**

# MAPPING THE STORY

*Mapping a story after reading it aids in understanding story structure.*

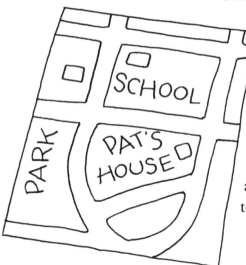

**WHAT YOU'LL NEED:** book with settings that shift several times, paper, pencil

Begin by having the child read the book. Then ask the child to write down where the story begins and every location described in the book. Help the child make a story map, showing the locations by labeling them (school, someone's house, park, and so on). For an additional challenge, add arrows showing the route the main character takes to go to these locations.

**39**

# BOOK REVIEW

▼▼▼▼▼▼▼▼▼▼▼▼▼▼▼▼▼▼▼▼▼▼▼▼▼▼▼▼

*The child will practice critical reading skills while preparing a book review.*

**WHAT YOU'LL NEED:** book the child has not read

Invite the child to read a new book. Discuss with the child all the things he or she liked and did not like about the book. Make a list of likes and dislikes. For a more challenging activity, encourage the child to write a short review of the book based on the list. Invite the child to share the review with you for further discussion.

# SNOWY DAY FUN

 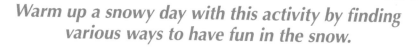

**40**

*Warm up a snowy day with this activity by finding various ways to have fun in the snow.*

**WHAT YOU'LL NEED:** *The Snowy Day* by Ezra Jack Keats, white glue, pencil, dark paper, blunt scissors, construction paper

Read the book aloud together. Discuss all kinds of ways to have fun in snow. One way is to make a snowman. Help the child make a snowman on paper by drawing the outline of a snowman on the dark paper. Fill in the outline with white glue. Allow the glue to dry. Cut out various items, such as a hat, a broom, and gloves, and glue those in place. Vary this by drawing several sizes of snowmen on the paper and labeling them by size or other characteristics.

# BACKPACK BOOKS

*Backpack books bring characters to life as the child practices telling the story from a character's point of view.*

**WHAT YOU'LL NEED:** favorite book, backpack or school bag, stuffed animal that relates to the book

Have the child keep the book and the stuffed animal in a backpack. Encourage the child to take it when going somewhere or for use at bedtime. Invite the child to read the book to the stuffed animal. Another time, have the child pretend to be the stuffed animal, reading to you in the animal's "voice."

# ACTIVITY TWIST

Add writing materials to the backpack and invite the child to create letters or notes to and from the characters in the story.

# COLOR WORDS

*Making books about color is a fun and productive activity for the child to reinforce color words.*

**WHAT YOU'LL NEED:** picture book showing color words, paints, paintbrush, paper

Read the book aloud together. Then read the book again, pointing out the color words on the pages. Talk about how the illustrator and/or author used color and words to show what the words, such as *red,* mean. Decide what would make a good color book. Then invite the child to use paints to make a book. Help the child print the color words to label the colors.

# FAIRY-TALE CHALLENGE

*In this activity, different versions of fairy tales are discussed.*

**WHAT YOU'LL NEED:** 3 versions of one fairy tale, such as *Goldilocks and the Three Bears* or *Cinderella*

Read aloud the three versions of the same fairy tale together. Then discuss the beginnings. Compare how the retellers started the stories. Did they all start with "Once upon a time"? Did some have short sentences and some have long? Did some make the beginning serious and others start with humor? How do the illustrations differ?

Continue by discussing the rest of the story. Invite the child to compare illustrations, portrayals of the characters, how the story ends, and so on.

# FLEAS AND FLIES

*Alliteration always appeals! Sample some with this poetry collection.*

**WHAT YOU'LL NEED:** *The Random House Book of Poetry for Children* selected by Jack Prelutsky

Alliteration occurs when a series of words begin with the same letter, such as "bees buzz busily." Many of the poems in the section called "Alphabet Stew" have alliteration.

Share several poems with the child. Then discuss the use of alliteration and how it affects the poems. Make up some poems that have alliteration and start a personal poetry book. Share with others.

# BOOKMARKS

**45**

*These decorative bookmarks will help the child keep his or her place when reading a favorite book.*

**WHAT YOU'LL NEED:** favorite book, paper, card stock, blunt scissors, markers, yarn

Have the child read the book. Then cut the card stock into the size of a bookmark. Explain to the child how a bookmark not only marks a page but can also be used to summarize the book. Invite the child to write a summary of the book on a sheet of paper before writing it on the bookmark. Remember to choose words carefully so they fit in the small area. Once the summary has been written on the bookmark, invite the child to decorate it with markers and colorful yarn.

**46**

# HERO POSTER

*Making posters is a creative activity that encourages reading and writing.*

**WHAT YOU'LL NEED:** book with a make-believe hero, construction paper, poster paints or markers

Begin by having the child read the book. Encourage him or her to write down several interesting facts from the book. Then help the child plan all the components of a promotional poster for the book. For example, the poster might include famous moments, heroic qualities, challenges, photographs or drawings, and so forth. Be ready for some poster-creating fun!

# SING-ALONG FUN

**47**

*Inspire the young lyricist by using familiar songs.*

**WHAT YOU'LL NEED:** simple songs, paper, pencil

Choose a simple song, such as "Skip to My Lou." Sing it with the child. Don't worry if you don't have a beautiful voice! Then discuss the rhymes in the song. Talk about how to create new verses. Invite the child to write some new verses. Then read them, learn to sing them, and teach the song to others.

# COMPREHENSION CAPERS

Comprehension is about understanding ideas through sentences. The activities contained in this chapter are designed to help the child develop into a confident reader who comprehends what is being read. The child will explore the main idea and supporting details while giggling through Opening a Can of Worms, sharpen skills for retelling stories while making and using Envelope Puppets, and get a real taste of sequencing in Peanut Butter Roll-Ups. Additional activities are sure to generate enthusiasm for reading while building skills necessary for comprehension.

## STACK-A-STORY

48

*Busy hands will love the challenge of this story-building activity.*

**WHAT YOU'LL NEED:** 3-6 cardboard boxes, poster paints, paintbrushes

Set out boxes and materials for painting. Discuss the main events in a story you and the child have recently read together. Then assist the child in painting a story scene on each cardboard box. When the boxes are dry, have the child stack them in rows so they can be read from left to right. Invite the child to retell the story in sequential order.

# FACE IT!

**49**

*Get ready to "Face It!" as the child explores character expressions.*

SHE LOOKS HAPPY.

**WHAT YOU'LL NEED:** old magazines, blunt scissors, clear tape or glue, construction paper, markers

Invite the child to cut out pictures of faces from old magazines. The faces on the people should show specific expressions, such as happy, sad, angry, scared, excited, worried, or surprised. Have the child glue or tape the most expressive faces on colored construction paper. Then invite the child to add speech balloons with words the child thinks the people are saying or thinking.

**50**

# STORY HANGER

*Door hangers are not only for clothes; they can also be used to tell about a favorite storybook.*

**WHAT YOU'LL NEED:** blunt scissors, pencil, poster board, favorite book or story, felt-tip pens

Draw and cut out a door hanger similar to the one shown here. Be sure to cut out a hanger large enough to fit on a doorknob. Then encourage the child to write the title and author of a favorite book or story as well as draw a picture or write a sentence about it on the front of the poster board hanger.

CLIFFORD THE BIG DOG BY

Invite the child to place the hanger on a friend's or sibling's door, desk, or coat hook to encourage them to read the book, too.

# OPENING A CAN OF WORMS

**51**

*The child will wiggle and giggle while learning about main ideas and supporting details.*

**WHAT YOU'LL NEED:** tin can, construction paper, precut worms made from construction paper or poster board, clear tape, felt-tip pens, familiar story

Begin by wrapping a tin can with construction paper and securing it with tape. Write the main idea of a familiar story on the outside of the tin can, turning the can around so the child will not see it. On each precut worm, write a supporting detail to the story, then place all the worms in the can. Explain that supporting details are pieces of information that work together to help tell the main idea. You may also want to discuss how each story has a beginning, middle, and end. Invite the child to pick worms from the can, read the sentences on them, and identify the main idea of the story.

# GREETING CARDS

**52**

*Build an understanding of author's purpose, audience, and main idea while creating a friendly greeting.*

**WHAT YOU'LL NEED:** construction paper, clear tape or glue, blunt scissors, art and craft scraps, felt-tip pens, envelopes, postage stamps

Discuss a list of greetings together, such as hello, get well, congratulations, happy birthday, and I love you. Invite the child to write a greeting on a piece of construction paper, and decorate it with art scraps. Then have the child explain who the card is for (the audience), why it was made (author's purpose), and what greeting was written (main idea). You may want to assist the child with addressing and stamping the envelopes to mail.

# HANGING IT OUT TO DRY

**53**

*The child can retell a favorite story while hanging homemade socks on a clothesline.*

**WHAT YOU'LL NEED:** clothesline, clothespins, tagboard, blunt scissors, markers, favorite book or story

String a clothesline across one corner of the room and clip several clothespins to it. Next have the child cut out three to six socks from tagboard and illustrate a scene from a familiar story on each. You may wish to provide a copy of the book or story for the child to refer to while working. Then have the child hang the completed socks on the clothesline in sequential order while retelling the story.

## ACTIVITY TWIST

As a fun, bet-I've-got-you-thinking variation of this activity, mix up the socks and hang them in random order on the clothesline. Challenge the child to find the mistake and correct it.

# BLAST OFF!

▼▼▼▼▼▼▼▼▼▼▼▼▼▼▼▼▼▼▼▼▼▼▼▼▼▼▼

**54**

*10–9–8–7–6–5–4–3–2–1 BLAST OFF into reading comprehension with this rocket construction project.*

**WHAT YOU'LL NEED:** white paper cut into long strips, paper towel tube, 6-inch circle of blue construction paper, blunt scissors, clear tape, pencil, string

First cut a slit in the middle of the circle of blue construction paper. Then wrap and tape the paper circle to make a cone. Tape the cone to the top of the paper towel tube. Next invite the child to write the main idea of a favorite story on the body of the rocket (cardboard tube). Help the child write supporting details on the strips of white paper. Then have the child tape the strips of paper to the bottom of the rocket before hanging it with string from the ceiling.

**55**

# CHARACTER MOBILE

■ ▪ ■ ▪ ■ ▪ ■ ▪ ■ ▪ ■

*The child will become familiar with characters in a favorite story when creating a character mobile.*

**WHAT YOU'LL NEED:** 10×12-inch polystyrene plate, 8×14-inch strands of yarn, cutout poster board shapes, hole punch, markers, paper, favorite book or story, clear tape or glue

Begin by inviting the child to draw and label pictures of each character from a favorite story. Help the child tape or glue the pictures on individual poster board shapes. Punch one hole in the top of each shape and enough holes around the outside edge of the plate to accompany the shapes. Have the child thread yarn strands through the shapes and plates. Then tie them together so the shapes dangle from the plate. Hang the finished mobile in a room for all to see.

# **56** Hoop It Up

*Hoop it up with this sockball-tossing game of skill, poetry, and real or make-believe story events.*

**WHAT YOU'LL NEED:** 2 small, clean waste baskets, paper, clear tape, markers, balled-up socks, favorite books or poems

Before beginning, mark a line on the floor with masking tape. Place two small garbage cans about 12 feet from the line. Place labels marked REAL and MAKE BELIEVE on the sides of the cans. Set out a pile of clean balled-up socks.

To play, invite the child to read favorite passages from books or poems you have recently read or enjoyed. Ask the child to decide whether the events and characters are real or not. Allow time for the child to answer. Once an answer is given, have the child stand behind the line and toss a balled-up sock into the appropriate basket. When all the socks have been tossed, count them to see how many characters the child thought were real or make-believe.

# **1-2-3 Surprise!** **57**

*Act out new endings for favorite 1-2-3 stories.*

Act out a story with the child in which something happens one, two, or three times, and then has a surprise ending. For added fun, make up a new surprise ending. The following are some suggestions:

*Goldilocks and the Three Bears*    *Jack and the Beanstalk*

*The Three Little Pigs*    *Three Billy Goats Gruff*

# RIDDLE DEE DEE

**58**

*The child strengthens comprehension skills while hopping through riddles.*

**WHAT YOU'LL NEED:** 3–5 hula hoops, riddle book

Lay three to five hula hoops on the floor, one in front of the other, as shown here. Then read a riddle. Next invite the child to solve the riddle. If the child answers the riddle correctly, he or she can hop into the first hula hoop. If the child is unable to answer the riddle, he or she cannot advance. Switch roles with the child when he or she reaches the last hoop.

# PICTURE THIS!

**59**

*The child takes on the role of a photographer while "taking pictures" of similar household objects.*

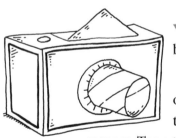

**WHAT YOU'LL NEED:** 4×6-inch cardboard box, cardboard tube, foil, blunt scissors, 3×5 index cards, crayons, construction paper

Cut a 3½-inch piece from a cardboard tube. Cut four 1-inch slits around one end of the tube. Bend the slits out. Place the cardboard box on the table with the open side facing you. The open side is the back of the camera. Tape the tube to the bottom of the box. Cover the box with foil, leaving the back open. Draw shutters, lenses, and buttons on construction paper, cut them out, and glue them to the front and sides of the camera.

Next invite the child to "take photos" of pairs of household objects that are similar, such as objects that are the same shape. (For photos, draw pictures on index cards and place inside the camera.) At the end of the activity, remove the pictures from the camera and display for others to see.

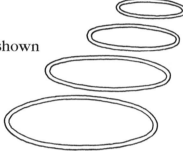

# DUCK, DUCK, CATEGORIES

**60**

*Try this twist on the familiar game Duck, Duck, Goose by using categories.*

Have players sit in a circle on the floor. Then the player chosen to be IT selects a category, such as food, and proceeds around the circle tapping players on the head, naming an object in the category—a different object for each head tapped. When an object is named that does not fit in the category, the player whose head has just been tapped stands up and the chase is on! IT tries to run around the circle and sit in the empty space before being tagged by the tapped player. If IT makes it successfully, the other player becomes IT and play starts over, using the same category. If IT is tagged, he or she retains the role of IT and a new game begins.

**61**

# BAG-O-BOOKS

*Share and discuss favorite books and stories with the child in this contagious activity.*

**WHAT YOU'LL NEED:** backpack, favorite books, sticky notes

Invite the child to select a few favorite books he or she has either read or wants to read, and put them in a backpack. Encourage the child to read the book and attach sticky notes on the books with comments. The child may wish to comment on which book was a favorite, which books were written by a favorite author, and which books had interesting illustrations. The child may also tag a favorite page in each book or a story event that was particularly funny or interesting.

After the child has finished reading the bag-o-books, it is your turn to read and make comments. After you have finished reading the books, discuss the comments. Encourage the child to send the bag-o-books on to a friend, sibling, or another adult, and have each of the readers make comments.

# REPORT CARDS

*Make a mock report card to see if characters in favorite stories and books make the grade.*

62

**WHAT YOU'LL NEED:** construction paper, felt-tip pen

On a folded piece of construction paper, invite the child to make a report card with at least three areas for grading a story character. Include the following areas: helpfulness, attitude, sense of humor, completing assignments, following rules, and being on time. The report is not complete until the child "grades" the character in each of the selected areas. The child may even find it necessary to request a conference with the character's parents. If so, this should be noted on the report card, too.

63

# FUNNY DAYS

*The calendar will never be the same with this fun, day-renaming activity.*

**WHAT YOU'LL NEED:** calendar, posterboard, markers

Before beginning this activity, look at a calendar together and point out the following to the child: the month and year, days of the week, numbers for the days, and special events. After setting out posterboard and markers, invite the child to design a calendar for one week, like the example shown here. Have the child create new names for the days of the week based on his or her scheduled activities or how he or she feels about a particular day. For example, the child may rename Saturday, *Soccerday,* and rename Friday, *Funday.*

# 64 CHOW DOWN

*Explore a character's likes and dislikes in this
sure-to-make-you-hungry activity.*

**WHAT YOU'LL NEED:** paper plates, old magazines, blunt
scissors, clear tape or glue, favorite books

Have the child look through a collection of favorite books and
select one with a main character he or she is particularly fond of.
Invite the child to explain why he or she likes the character. Then
help the child plan a meal for the character. Start by cutting out
pictures of various foods from old magazines. Then attach the pictures to a paper plate to show
what will be served. If the character is an animal, help the child research the kind of food the animal
eats. The child may also wish to create a just-for-fun menu that is sure to whet his or her favorite
character's appetite.

# STORY PIZZA 65

*Slice, mix, sort, and arrange pieces of a story as
you create a delicious story pizza.*

**WHAT YOU'LL NEED:** pie pan, cardboard circle (same diameter as the pie pan) blunt scissors,
marker

Pretend that the cardboard circle is a large pizza. Invite the child to imagine what toppings the
pizza would have on it and how it would look, smell, and taste. Then cut the cardboard pie into three
equal slices. Discuss with the child events at the beginning, the middle, and the end of a favorite
story. Next have the child draw a picture or write at least one sentence that tells about each event
on a separate piece of pizza. Then have the child put the slices of pizza in the pie pan in the correct
order, working clockwise, while retelling the story.

# NEWS OF THE DAY!

66

*Explore main ideas as the child writes headlines
for a day's events and activities.*

**WHAT YOU'LL NEED:** magnetic letters, magnetic surface or refrigerator door

Recall the events the child was involved in on a particular day. Discuss the most important and the most memorable events. Which event or events would other people want to know about?

Page through a newspaper together. Point out the headlines to the child. Explain that a headline is used to provide a glimpse of what's in the article and entice the reader to read the article.

Display uppercase and lowercase magnetic letters on a magnetic surface. Let the child manipulate the letters freely for a few minutes, then invite the child to arrange the letters to create a headline describing a highlight of the day.

## ACTIVITY TWIST

For an additional challenge, point to particular headline in the newspaper and ask the child to guess what the story is about. See how accurate the child and the headline are.

# A Box-o'-Socks

**67**

*Laundry day is a wash with this sorting activity that engages the child in critical thinking.*

**WHAT YOU'LL NEED:** box or laundry basket, socks

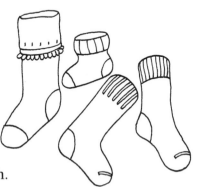

Collect socks in a variety of sizes, colors, patterns, and types. Check out some used clothing stores if you need more of a variety. Then have the child sort the socks into several specific categories. For example, sort first by color then by size. Next try sorting by function, such as socks for a baseball player, soccer player, snow skier, or maybe a ballerina. Invite the child to think of new categories for sorting socks. See how many different sorting ideas the child can come up with.

**68**

# Event Hangers

*Understanding cause and effect relationships in reading is made simple with this creative activity.*

**WHAT YOU'LL NEED:** paper-covered clothes hangers, old magazines, favorite story, stapler, yarn, hole punch, markers, tagboard, blunt scissors, clear tape or glue

Begin by having the child read a favorite story. Then invite the child to draw a picture on the paper covering a hanger that shows an important event in the story. Next have the child draw or cut out pictures from old magazines showing what caused the event to happen. Glue or tape the pictures on tagboard cutouts. Help the child punch a hole in the top of each tagboard shape and the bottom of the hanger, string yarn through the holes, tie, and hang the cutouts from the clothes hanger. Display for others to see.

# ENVELOPE PUPPETS

**69**

*The imaginative child will love creating these
animated story puppets.*

**WHAT YOU'LL NEED:** 6½×9½-inch manila envelopes, blunt scissors, clear tape or glue, poster paints, paintbrushes, art and craft scraps

Set out all materials. To make the puppets, carefully cut off the top flap of the manila envelopes. (Quantities will vary according to the amount of puppets you and the child want to make.) Then invite the child to paint faces on the envelopes. Have the child glue or tape odds and ends of art scraps on the envelopes to create puppets resembling characters from a favorite story or book. Have the child put his or her hands inside the envelope puppets. The child can then move his or her arms up and down and side by side to show action. Encourage the child to use the finished puppets for retelling the story or for other dramatic play.

## ACTIVITY TWIST

For an additional activity, help the child create a puppet stage. Paint a cardboard box with poster paints and use it as the setting of the story.

# 70

## Blue Ribbon

• • • • • • • • • • • • • • • • • • • • • • • • •

*HIP, HIP, HOORAY! You'll be cheering, too, for the heroes in this rewarding activity about characters.*

**WHAT YOU'LL NEED:** 2 blue ribbon streamers, blue and yellow construction paper, blunt scissors, clear tape or glue, markers

FIRST PLACE! YOU'RE A WINNER! FUNNIEST DOG! HERO! YOU'RE NUMBER 1!

Discuss different ways to describe a person or an animal that has accomplished an outstanding achievement. Then invite the child to design and create a blue ribbon award for a favorite story character. Explain that the award may be for kindness, hard work, courage, or any other reason the child thinks is noteworthy. Create the ribbon from construction paper and blue ribbon streamers. Suggest that the ribbon have the name of the character printed on it and why the award was given.

## Cereal Treat

# 71

▼▼▼▼▼▼▼▼▼▼▼▼▼▼▼▼▼▼▼▼▼▼▼▼▼▼▼▼

*Guess your cereal surprise while the child learns about character traits.*

**WHAT YOU'LL NEED:** empty cereal box, sticky notes, small object, sandwich bag

Begin by having the child place a small, clean object, or "prize," inside a plastic sandwich bag, then place it in an empty cereal box. Make sure the child keeps the identity of the object a secret. Next invite the child to write words that describe the object on sticky notes. Attach the sticky notes to the box.

Now it's up to you to guess the prize after reading the descriptive labels. Then dig into the box and pull out the prize to see if you are correct.

# THEME DOMINOES

*This version of Dominoes is a matching activity based on the popular children's game.*

**WHAT YOU'LL NEED:** tagboard, old magazines, blunt scissors, clear tape or glue

Decide on a category, such as furniture, animals, or transportation, and make dominoes that depict several objects in the chosen category. The dominoes can be made by cutting and taping or gluing small pictures from old magazines on precut tagboard rectangles. Explain to the child that pictures of each object should appear on at least three dominoes. Then play dominoes using the following rules of the traditional game.

Turn dominoes facedown on a table. Each player picks five dominoes and places the pieces faceup in front of them. Players then take turns placing one domino at a time on the board. A domino may only be placed on the board if one of its halves matches a domino already on the board. For

example, if the domino on the board has a picture of a moving van, a player can only place a matching domino on the board. Matching dominoes can be placed end to end or end to side. If a player does not have a match, he or she must pick from the remaining dominoes until a match is found. The first player to run out of dominoes is the winner.

# SCAVENGER HUNT

*A keen eye for detail will help the young detective when searching for items in this scavenger hunt.*

**WHAT YOU'LL NEED:** bag with handle, paper, crayons or pencils

Have the child number a piece of paper from 1 to 5. Then invite the child to draw the following pictures next to the corresponding number on the paper.

1. desk
2. envelope
3. tree branch
4. kitchen drawer
5. sewing basket

Next have the child go on a scavenger hunt around the room, around the house, or in other safe locations to collect something that can be found in or on each object on the child's list. For example, the child's collection may include a pencil (from a desk), a stamp (from an envelope), a leaf (from a tree branch), a spoon (from a kitchen drawer), and a button (from a sewing basket). If necessary, have the child return the items after the scavenger hunt.

# FLIP, FLAP, FLOP

**74**

*The child will flip while uncovering
directions in sequence!*

**WHAT YOU'LL NEED:** 12×18-inch piece of paper folded in half lengthwise, blunt scissors, crayons or markers

Invite the child to describe steps in a familiar process, such as preparing a bowl of cereal, building a wooden block castle, or brushing teeth. Help the child cut three or more flaps in the paper, depending on the number of steps in the process. (There should be one flap for each step.) Cut from the edge of the paper toward the fold. Then have the child write the steps on the underside of the sheet, one step underneath each flap. Then write the corresponding numeral (1, 2, 3) to show the order of the steps on the covering flap. Have the child turn up each flap as he or she describes the sequence.

**75**

# STEP BY STEP

*While learning how to formulate questions, the child
will enhance story comprehension.*

Begin by having one player take on the role of a character from a favorite story both players have read. Next have the other player try to guess the identity of the character by asking a maximum of ten questions that can be answered "yes" or "no." For example, suggest the following: Are you a person? Are you an animal? Do you have fur? Did you ever blow down a straw house?

Take turns with different characters and see how many questions it takes to guess the character. The player who correctly identities the character in the least amount of questions is the winner.

 **76**

# PEANUT BUTTER ROLL-UPS

*Making these tasty, no-bake snacks is a great way for the child to practice following directions.*

**WHAT YOU'LL NEED:** 2 tablespoons powered sugar, 2 tablespoons powdered milk, 4 tablespoons peanut butter, ¼ cup pecan pieces, wooden spoon, mixing bowl

Have the child follow these simple directions to make an easy, nutritious snack.

1. Put 2 tablespoons of powdered sugar in a bowl.
2. Add 2 tablespoons of powdered milk.
3. Add 4 tablespoons of peanut putter.
4. Add ¼ cup pecan pieces.
5. Mix.
6. Roll the mixture into golf-ball-sized circles.
7. Put the roll-ups in the refrigerator until cold.
8. Take out of refrigerator and enjoy a tasty, nutritious snack.

## 77 TOTEM POLES

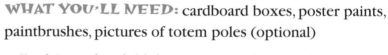

*Learn about cultures and tradition while building totem poles that reflect important images from a story.*

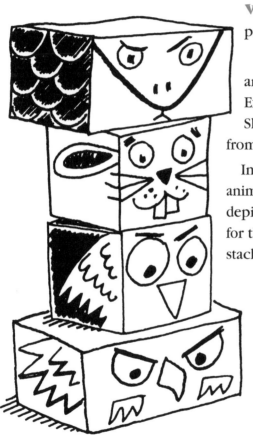

**WHAT YOU'LL NEED:** cardboard boxes, poster paints, paintbrushes, pictures of totem poles (optional)

Explain to the child that a totem pole is a tall pole on which an animal or other images from nature are carved or painted. Explain that totem poles are symbolic and often tell a story. Show examples of authentic Native American totem poles from picture books, if possible.

Invite the child to read a nonfiction story or article about animals or nature. Then help the child paint cardboard boxes depicting important images from the story. Allow plenty of time for the boxes to dry before moving them. Then have the child stack the boxes one on top of the other to resemble a totem pole.

# 78   IF-THEN CARDS

*Challenge the child's thinking skills with this game of cause-and-effect relationships.*

**WHAT YOU'LL NEED:** ten 3×5 index cards, blunt scissors, markers, basket

Before you begin, cut ten index cards in half. Write the words IF on the top part of the card and the word THEN on the bottom part. Give the child all of the cards. Invite the child to write or draw pictures on each set of cards, using the IF-THEN formula. Suggest using ideas from a familiar story or rhyme. You may wish to create one set of cards for the child as an example, such as:

If I jump in the puddle

Then I will get wet

To play the game, have the child scramble the cards. Challenge the child to match tops and bottoms to show a complete, reasonable idea.

# CHARACTER CHARADES   79

*The child will growl like a big wolf or scold like a mother hen while acting out favorite story characters.*

After reading a favorite story together, invite the child to choose a character from the story to pantomime. Have the child focus on the character's actions, feelings, emotions, specific physical traits, and role within the story. Invite the child to use a particular scene from the story when pantomiming. Try to guess what character is being pantomimed.

# SING ALONG

*Sing along as the child uses imagination to act out songs that tell a story.*

**WHAT YOU'LL NEED:** tape player and cassettes of familiar songs (optional)

Sing along with familiar songs that tell a story, such as "The Farmer in the Dell," "There was an Old Lady Who Swallowed a Fly," "In a Cabin in the Woods," "Five Little Ducks," "On Top of Spaghetti," and "Little Bunny Foo Foo." Invite the child to act out a character in the song while singing. Point out that most songs tell a story with special events or actions that happen at the beginning, the middle, and the end. Some of the songs end with an event that will make you laugh.

## ACTIVITY TWIST

Using the song "The Farmer in the Dell," have the child create new verses about the Farmer. Then invite the child to act out those new verses while singing the words.

**81**

# SHADOW PLAY

*The child will enjoy imaginative storytelling through these shadow puppets.*

**WHAT YOU'LL NEED:** bright flashlight, blank wall

Cast a bright light against a light-colored wall. Sit between the light and the wall and demonstrate how to make shadow puppets by manipulating your hands to create the desired shadow images. For example, form a rabbit using the thumb to hold down the last two fingers on the same hand and having the pointer and index fingers straight up, slightly apart.

Invite the child to use imagination to create other shadow puppets on the wall. Then encourage the child to make up a story about these shadow characters and perform the show for others.

# QUICK DRAW!

**82**

*This observation and classification activity will endlessly amuse the child.*

**WHAT YOU'LL NEED:** markers, large sheets of paper

Have the child draw four animals (or other objects) on a piece of paper, making sure that three have similar characteristics. The child may want to start with pictures of a zebra, tiger, coral snake, and a bear. Let the child decide which three are alike and in what ways. You'll notice in the example shown that three have stripes. It is also true that three of the animals shown have four legs.

Challenge the child to "fix" the fourth animal or object to make it fit in the group. Be prepared for some silly drawings!

# PRONOUN BINGO

83

*The child will have fun playing this familiar game of wits, luck, and learning about pronouns.*

**WHAT YOU'LL NEED:** cardboard, felt-tip pens, game markers (beans, paper squares, bottle caps)

| B | I | N | G | O |
|---|---|---|---|---|
| HE | SHE | THEY | IT | WE |
| ME | | | | |
| | | | | |
| | | | | |
| | | | | |

Before beginning the game, make a cardboard Bingo game board. Write a pronoun—such as *he, she, we, they, it*—in each square. (The example shown is only a partially completed board. Make sure that every board is different.) To play the game, call out names of people, objects, or animals, both singular and plural, and have each player cover the square containing the corresponding pronoun. The first player to cover five squares in a row is the winner.

84

# FINGER PAINT FOLLIES

*These tasty replacements for fingerpaint provide an easy-to-clean-up and fun-to-use method to paint predictions.*

**WHAT YOU'LL NEED:** whipped cream or ready-made pudding, sponges, pail of water, smock

Invite the child to spread whipped cream or pudding on the top of a clean kitchen table, preferably one with a surface that can easily be cleaned with sponges and water. Then read a nursery rhyme that is unfamiliar to the child. At some point in the rhyme, pause and ask the child to finger-paint a picture to show what he or she predicts will happen next.

Repeat this activity with other nursery rhymes. Have the child "erase" the previous drawing by rubbing over it with his or her hands. The child can then sponge the excess pudding or whipped cream off the table when finished.

# RAIN DANCE

*Defining main ideas becomes a lively performance when a little song and dance is done.*

Sing the song "The Eensy Weensy Spider" together. Discuss the main idea of the song. Then work with the child to create a dance showing the spider going up and down the water spout. Have the child perform the dance while the song is being played or sung. Repeat this activity using other familiar songs such as "Frosty the Snowman," "I'm a Little Teapot," and "Oh Where, Oh Where Has My Little Dog Gone?"

For added fun, invite other children to add details to the song by dancing or pantomiming the parts of the sun shining, the rain falling, flowers opening, and so on.

# WORD QUESTS

Children are naturally curious about their environment. They use their keen eyes and developing senses of taste, smell, touch, and hearing to explore the world around them. The language they hear associated with their experiences forms the foundation for their listening, speaking, reading, and writing vocabularies. In this chapter, vocabulary instruction comes alive for children, motivating even the most reluctant learners through engaging games and activities. Whether the child plays Antonym Checkers, is amused with Compound Caterpillars, or just gets tickled with Mouse in a Blouse, you can be sure he or she will have fun while improving basic vocabulary skills.

## 86 ABC ACTION

*A, B, C, D, E, F, Gee, it's fun to pantomime action words with this up-and-at-'em action activity.*

**WHAT YOU'LL NEED:** paper, pencil, construction paper, crayons or markers

What do the words *run, skip, climb, eat, plant, fly,* and *sing* have in common? They are action words, or verbs. Make a list of action words together, then ask the child to choose a word from the list to pantomime. Invite the child to illustrate the action by writing the word on a piece of paper, making the first letter perform the action. For example, a child may write the word *sing* in which the *s* is singing, or write the word *run* and in which the *r* appears to be running.

# STICK UPS

87

*Forming words from mixed-up letters is an exciting and educational way for the child to learn story vocabulary.*

**WHAT YOU'LL NEED:** magnetic letters, magnetic surface, favorite book or story

Select an interesting word from a favorite book or story and collect magnetic letters to make that word. Use a safe working surface to display the letters, such as a magnetic board, refrigerator door, front of a washing machine, or metal file cabinet. Then scramble the letters. Next invite the child to unscramble the letters to create the known word. You may want to provide clues to help the child guess the word. Continue the activity with more words from the story.

88

# TIC-TAC-TOE A WORD

*Try this new twist on the popular children's game.*

**WHAT YOU'LL NEED:** paper, felt-tip pens

Make two Tic-Tac-Toe boards, one for each player, by drawing three rows of three squares on a piece of paper. The squares should be relatively large, at least 1½×1½ inches. Next the players should decide on nine words, perhaps theme-related words (such as foods, animals, favorite story characters) or recently learned vocabulary words, and write them in random order in the squares on each of the Tic-Tac-Toe boards.

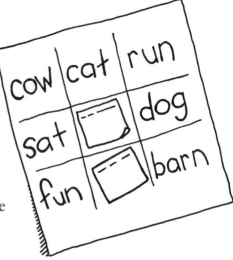

The game is played as in regular Tic-Tac-Toe, except here the player must say the word and use it in a sentence before it can be covered. The first player to cover three words in a row—either across, down, or at an angle—wins the game.

# PUFF, PUFF, TOOT, TOOT!

*Music and movement are an ideal and fun way
for the child to learn sound words.*

Sing the following chorus of the familiar song "Down by the Station" together. Then have the child repeat the words that imitate sounds in the song, such as *chug* and *toot*. Invite the child to mimic the sounds, emphasizing expression and body language, such as shuffling feet or moving the arm up and down while making a fist to simulate the motion that makes the sound "toot toot." Sing "Down By the Station" again, but this time have the child act out the sound words. Point out that more meaning is added to words when expressive voices and actions are used. Follow up by having the child list other sound words he or she knows.

Down by the station early in the morning,

See the little puffer bellies all in a row.

See the stationmaster turn the little handle,

Chug, chug, toot, toot,

Off we go!

## ACTIVITY TWIST

For an additional challenge, research the names for train cars. Find out what a puffer belly looks like and what it was used for.

## 90 · A, B, See It!

*Grab a pencil and a notebook and take the child on a walking field trip to explore words.*

**WHAT YOU'LL NEED:** notebook, pencil

Write a letter of the alphabet on the top of a piece of paper in a notebook. Give the notebook to the child and have him or her name the letter and indicate the sound for the letter. Next take the child on a letter walk, outside if possible. Instruct the child to look for words that begin with the letter on the paper. Then have the child copy the words into the notebook.

## Plant a Root Word · 91

*Learning root words has never been so enchanting as it is with this planting activity.*

**WHAT YOU'LL NEED:** polystyrene cups, dirt, craft sticks, construction paper, clear tape or glue, blunt scissors

Write a root word on a cup, and then fill it with dirt. You may want to use one of the following root word associated with planting: dig, plant, garden, water, seed, or grow. Invite the child to draw and cut out three to five construction paper flowers. Help the child glue or tape the paper cutouts onto craft sticks to make them sturdy. Have the child add ending letters (such as *ing* or *er*) or beginning letters (such as *un* or *pre*) to each root word to make new words, writing a new word on each flower. Finished flowers should be "planted" in the cup of dirt. Invite the child to make additional cups of flowers.

# PREFIX SLIP

*Create a bevy of different words with this charming approach to prefixes.*

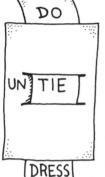

**WHAT YOU'LL NEED:** 5×8-inch rectangle of heavy paper or poster board, ruler, 12×3-inch strip of heavy paper or poster board, blunt scissors, markers

Help the child cut two horizontal slits in the rectangle of poster board, just above and below the center and to the right. The slits should be about four inches long and two inches apart. Then have the child write a prefix in the space to the left of the slits as shown. Common prefixes include but are not limited to: *un, re, dis, pre, de,* and *ex.* Then help the child write on the strip a list of words that can be added to the prefix to form a new word. Explain that by pulling the strip through the slits, the child can make and read new words with the designated prefix.

# BUBBLE GUM WORDS

*Every dentist will like these absolutely cavity-free bubble gum activities!*

What happens when you take one end of the bubble gum you are chewing and pull on it? It stretches! The same thing can happen to words. Words can get longer when extra letters are added to the beginning or the end. Write the word *and,* and show how to stretch it to make the words *hand* and *handcuff.* Then invite the child to stretch their own words from *and.* Use a child's dictionary if necessary.

# 94 ANTONYM CHECKERS

*How many kings can get crowned while playing this challenging game of checkers that uses antonyms?*

**WHAT YOU'LL NEED:** 24×24-inch poster board or cardboard square, ruler, markers, checkers or large red and black buttons, crayons, masking tape

This game is played much like the original game of checkers, except that in order to be "crowned," a player can only land on a space with a corresponding *antonym*. For example, a player must move a checker marked "lovely" toward and eventually land on the red space marked "ugly" (the *antonym* of lovely) in order to be crowned. As in the original game, the player with the last remaining checker wins.

Begin by helping the child make a checkerboard. Draw an 8×8-inch grid on a piece of poster board or cardboard. Color the spaces red and black, alternating the colors as you go. Print the following words in the red squares on the first row of each player's home side: *big, sad, ugly, well.* Before starting the game, invite the child to select the color of checkers he or she would like to use as game pieces.

Next make two sets of game pieces. For each set, mark the game pieces by putting a piece of masking tape over each checker and writing one of the following words on each: *little, small, tiny, happy, joyful, glad, pretty, lovely, beautiful, ill, sick, unhealthy.* Then set the checkers on the red squares at each end of the board. Change the words periodically for continued play.

# POP, POP, POPCORN!

*Put the child's senses through the vocabulary test
with this popping good activity.*

**WHAT YOU'LL NEED:** threaded needles, popcorn, popcorn popper, oil, paper towels, construction paper squares

Begin by making some popcorn together. Invite the child to describe what he or she sees, hears, and smells while you are popping the popcorn. Record the words the child uses on paper squares. Snack on some of the popped popcorn while you and the child brainstorm other words that describe the treat, such as how it tastes. Then write those words on paper squares. Words to think about might include *salty, crunchy, pop, hot, white, munch,* and *yummy.*

Next help the child string some of the remaining popcorn together with the words on paper squares to create a decorative word bank. Display the completed strand in the room for a day or so to review the words. Then remove the popcorn from the strand and take outside for birds to enjoy.

# THE ALPHABET GAME

**96**

*You will love this ABC order game of wits and laughs.
It's great for a rainy day or a long trip.*

Invite the child to think of a word that begins with each letter of the alphabet. You may want to limit the search to a particular theme, such as words used in a current science study about insects or names of cities and states the child has learned in social studies. Have the child start with *A* and go in order. How far into the alphabet can the child go?

If the child is unable to think of a word that starts with a particular letter, suggest choosing a word that contains that letter.

# BEEP! BEEP!

**97**

*Investigate what makes common sounds and
experiment with ways to write them.*

**WHAT YOU'LL NEED:** tape recorder, butcher paper, paint, paintbrushes

Take a walk outside to record environmental sounds, such as a car honking its horn, birds chirping, sirens blaring, the wind howling, dogs barking, and so on. Later have the child listen to the recorded sounds and create words to describe them. Some examples might include: Beep! Beep!, Chirp! Chirp!, and Wr-r-r-r! Invite the child to paint the sound words in large letters on long pieces of butcher paper to create a vocabulary mural.

# PEEK-A-BOO

**98**

*Wits will be sharpened with this brain-teasing and thinking activity. Get ready!*

**WHAT YOU'LL NEED:** sticky notes, paper, pencil

Review a list of vocabulary words with the child. These may be words used in math, science, social studies, or reading. Write a sentence for each vocabulary word on the list. Then cover the vocabulary word in each sentence with a sticky note. Invite the child to read the sentences and try to determine which word is under the flap before lifting it and peeking to check.

What strategies did the child use to discover the word? Emphasize how listening to the other words in the sentence and thinking about words you know that will complete the sentence and make sense is a good strategy for finding the missing word.

**99**

# STRIKE!

*Have a ball with this simple milk jug bowling game, designed to reinforce recognition of sight words.*

**WHAT YOU'LL NEED:** 10 clean plastic milk jugs (½ gallon or quart), permanent markers, rubber ball

Have the child use permanent markers to write sight words on plastic milk jugs. Set up the jugs like bowling pins in rows of one, two, three, and four as shown. Invite the child to roll a ball down the lane and try to knock over the pins. The child gets one point for each pin he or she knocks over when the child reads the word on it.

# SHAPE WORDS

*Construct shape words that illustrate meanings of vocabulary words.*

**WHAT YOU'LL NEED:** markers or crayons, paper

Have the child choose vocabulary words that name objects, insects, or animals. Encourage creative thinking as the child writes the words so that the letters conform to the shape of the object. For example, the letters c-a-t-e-r-p-i-l-l-a-r may be written to take on the curved shapes of the insect, as in the example shown, or the word k-i-t-e may be written with tall letters to fill the diamond-shaped object.

## ACTIVITY TWIST

The interested child can take the project a step further and create a concrete poem. Explain that concrete poetry is when words in a poem are arranged to make a picture of what the poem is about.

# LABEL IT!

*By using labels, the child will identify and learn new words.*

101

**WHAT YOU'LL NEED:** posterboard, markers, square pieces of paper, clear tape

Explain to the child that pictures make it easier for us to understand a story or other information that we read. Also explain that some pictures have labels, or captions, next to them to name the parts of a picture. Invite the child to draw a picture of a favorite toy and label the parts he or she knows.

102

# DIAL-A-WORD

*Dialing these phone numbers will connect the child to some new vocabulary words.*

**WHAT YOU'LL NEED:** toy telephone (or picture of keypad with numbers and letters), paper, pencil

Looking at a toy telephone rotary dial or keypad, point to the numbers and name the letters that correspond to each number on the keypad. Explain to the child that the numbers 1 and 0 do not have corresponding letters. Make a list of vocabulary words and invite the child to "dial" each word. Have the child write down the corresponding number for each letter in the word.

# STAMP IT!

▼▼▼▼▼▼▼▼▼▼▼▼▼▼▼▼▼▼▼▼▼▼▼▼▼▼▼▼▼▼▼▼

*All the child needs to make and send this special birthday card is a little word study and a lot of love.*

**103**

**WHAT YOU'LL NEED:** sponge, corrugated cardboard or polystyrene, poster paints, folded construction paper cards, blunt scissors

Invite the child to make a birthday card for a special friend or family member while practicing vocabulary skills. Begin by talking about the greeting "Happy Birthday." Write the words in a place where the child can see them, and then spell them together. Help the child cut out letters *H, A, P, Y, B, I, R, T,* and *D* from sponge, corrugated cardboard, or polystyrene. Help dip the letters into a shallow dish of paint and then stamp the letters on folded cards to create the greeting *HAPPY BIRTHDAY.* When the greeting has dried, invite the child to decorate the card further and sign it before delivering it.

# CREATE A LOGO

**104**

▬ ▬ ▬ ▬ ▬ ▬ ▬ ▬ ▬ ▬ ▬ ▬ ▬ ▬

*Create a design that represent a specific idea or image about the creator.*

**WHAT YOU'LL NEED:** markers, heavy paper

Explain that a logo is a picture or design that is often accompanied by a few words. The logo tells something about a product that a company wants you to remember. Look for examples on sports equipment, electronic equipment, clothing, food, drinks, and so on.

Invite the child to design a personal logo. The child may wish to use one or more letters in his or her name as part of the design. Each logo should be accompanied by a name the child has created. Then think about practical ways to use logos, perhaps to mark possessions or as decorative imprints for clothing.

# CATEGORY CHALLENGE

*You'll need to sharpen your pencil and your wits for this word category game.*

**WHAT YOU'LL NEED:** paper, pencil

Have the child draw a grid on a piece of paper, six squares across and four squares down. Next choose four consonants and one vowel together and write them in boxes two through six across the top. Think of categories and list them down the left side. Then invite the child to try to complete the game board within a designated time period (3-10 minutes). The object is to come up with a word that begins with each letter in the top row and is part of the category listed.

|  | B | G | S | R | A |
|---|---|---|---|---|---|
| ANIMAL | bear | goat | snake | rat | ape |
| FOOD | banana |  | soup | radish | apple |
|  |  |  |  |  |  |

## 106 OH WHERE? OH WHERE?

*Help find a lost pet with this vocabulary-building activity about descriptive words.*

Sing the following familiar song with the child. For fun, invite the child to add body movements and sound effects, such as barking. Then help the child make a "wanted poster" for the lost dog, including a picture of the dog. Ask the child to describe what the dog looks like. Follow up by having the child change the words in the song to reflect another lost pet. Encourage the child to use descriptive words that may help others know what the lost pet looks like.

Oh where, oh where has my little dog gone?

Oh where, oh where can she be?

With her ears cut long and her tail cut short.

Oh where, oh where can she be?

## SHOE SOLE SIGHT WORD 107

*By matching these shoe soles, the child will practice "stepping into" sight words.*

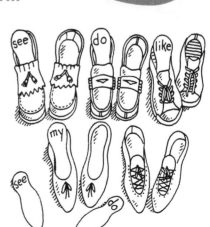

**WHAT YOU'LL NEED:** several pairs of shoes, marker, heavy paper precut in shoe sole shapes, list of sight words

On pairs of precut paper soles, write sight words, such as *do, my,* and *like*—the same word on each half of the pair. Place one "sole" of each word inside one shoe from each pair so the card is standing on end and the sight word is clearly visible. Set out the remaining soles and invite the child to place them in the empty shoe that matches the one with the same sight word.

## 108 CHEERY CHAINS

*Strengthen the child's vocabulary chain by learning new words associated with a familiar topic.*

**WHAT YOU'LL NEED:** 1½×8½-inch paper strips, clear tape or glue or stapler, crayons or markers, paper, pencil, reference books

Decide on a topic, such as food, animals, household objects, or the child's current social studies or science theme at school, and make a list of associated words. Then have the child write the words on the strips of paper. The child may also want to draw illustrations to go with each word. Provide glossaries, dictionaries, textbooks, and other materials as spelling aids.

Next invite the child to assemble the strips, or links, using glue or staples to make word chains. Chains can be strung across a room, made into individual necklaces, wrapped around bushes or trees, or draped around a doorway. Then review the words daily.

## PEASE PORRIDGE WHAT? 109

*An old nursery rhyme becomes the spark for a study of antonyms.*

Repeat the following Mother Goose rhyme, *Pease Porridge Hot.* Underline the words *hot* and *cold.* Ask the child how these words are related. (They are opposites.) Invite the child to substitute different pairs of word opposites, or *antonyms,* to make a silly version of the rhyme.

Pease porridge hot,  
pease porridge cold.  
Pease porridge in the pot  
nine days old.

Some like it hot,  
some like it cold.  
Some like it in the pot  
nine days old.

 **110**

# PIZZA PARTY!

*Here the budding young chef learns descriptive words while making a gigantic pizza!*

**WHAT YOU'LL NEED:** cardboard circle 24-36 inches in diameter, paper scraps, clear tape or glue, blunt scissors, large recipe card

To perk up a child's appetite, tempt him or her with this activity—making a gigantic pizza. Show the pizza crust (large cardboard circle) and have the child suggest ingredients to use for making pizza. (Use the example provided for suggestions.) Invite the child to list suggestions on the recipe card. Provide assistance with spelling as needed. The child will enjoy following the recipe, cutting and pasting or taping paper replicas of the ingredients, of course!

## GIGANTIC PIZZA

| | | |
|---|---|---|
| 20 slices of pepperoni | 50 cups of cheese | 5 anchovies |
| 2 green peppers | 1 giant pizza crust | 100 olives |
| 1 pineapple | 10 sausages | 12 cups of tomato sauce |
| 2 hams | 2 onions | |
| 30 tomatoes | 25 mushrooms | |

# ACTIVITY TWIST

Share recipes for making pizza from real cookbooks with the child. Compare the ingredients and the amounts used in the cookbook recipes to the recipe shown above. Did you forget any essential ingredients? If possible, follow the cookbook recipe to make a real pizza.

# WORD SCRABBLE

*This popular crossword game is a timeless way to practice vocabulary building.*

**WHAT YOU'LL NEED:** Scrabble game (board game or computer version)

Each player picks seven letters. Then players take turns and try to make words with the letters one player has chosen. Each player can pick one new letter for every letter played, or one new letter if unable to make a word. The first person to use all of the letters is the winner.

If you do not wish to have a "winner" for the game, have play continue until everyone's letters are used. Encourage teamwork by having players combine their letters to build new words.

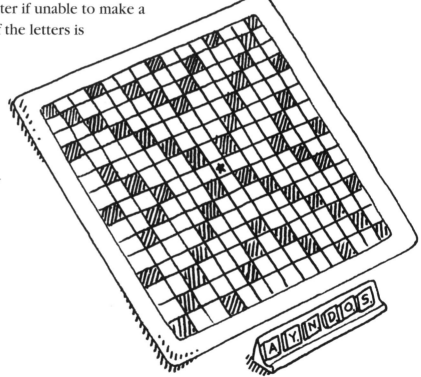

# JINGLE, JANGLE

*Children will love this action-packed verb game, and it will strengthen their imagination.*

Have the child write the first letter of his or her name. Then invite the child to write as many *verbs,* or action words, as he or she can think of that begin with the same letter. As a follow-up to the activity, see how many *nouns*—names of people, places, or things—the child can list.

# COMPOUND CATERPILLARS

*The child will enjoy this interesting take on compound words while making construction paper caterpillars.*

**WHAT YOU'LL NEED:** 11×4-inch construction paper caterpillar cutouts, markers or crayons

Take turns naming compound words. Explain that a compound word is two separate words that are combined to make one word. Write the words on a chart. Then set out precut paper caterpillars, similar to those shown here. The child can then fold the left and right ends of the caterpillar cutouts in to meet at the middle. Have the child write words on the outside flaps of the cutout—one word for each flap—that make up a particular compound word from the chart. Next have the child unfold the flaps and write the compound word on the inside of the caterpillar. Invite the child to share the finished work with others.

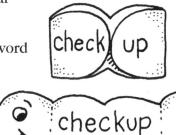

# In Another Tongue

*The child can expand his or her horizons with this multicultural language activity using counting words.*

Learn to count to ten in a language other than the one you use every day. Use a dictionary of the language chosen for correct pronunciation, or look for the words in books from the library.

| SPANISH | | JAPANESE | |
|---|---|---|---|
| uno | seis | ichi | roku |
| dos | siete | ni | shichi |
| tres | ocho | san | hachi |
| cuatro | nueve | shi | ku |
| cinco | diez | go | ju |

# Mouse in a Blouse

**115**

*Bet you can't play Mouse in a Blouse without laughing. Ready, set, try it!*

**WHAT YOU'LL NEED:** paper, pencil, crayons

Invite the child to draw animals dressed in clothes. The only rule is that the animal's name must rhyme with the name of the clothing. How about a goat in a coat? A kitten wearing a mitten? A dog in clogs? Or try to hold back a giggle when you see a mouse in a blouse or ants in pants! Have the child write a title for each dressed animal.

**116**

# DOGGIE, DOGGIE

*Defining words is not so r-r-r-uff when the child is engaged in this dog-and-bone game.*

**WHAT YOU'LL NEED:** 8–12 bone-shaped paper cutouts, markers

Write vocabulary words on bone-shaped cutouts. Sit on the floor facing each other to play the game "Doggie, Doggie, Who's Got Your Bone?" While one player chants "Doggie, Doggie, Who's Got Your Bone?" the other player sits with the bones turned over so that the writing is facedown. When the "doggie" finishes the chant, he or she picks up one of the bones and reads the word. If the "doggie" can correctly define the word, he or she gets to keep the bone and play continues. If not, the "doggie" must give the other player a chance to collect some bones.

# VOCABULARY SEED PACKS

**117**

*Little seeds of knowledge can grow into a garden of information with this vocabulary-rich project.*

**WHAT YOU'LL NEED:** 3×5 index cards, markers, seed packs

Have the child look at some real seed packs. Then invite the child to design a seed pack for something they'd like to grow. Have the child draw a colorful picture of the plant on the front of the pack and label it. Invite the child to write a descriptive sentence about the plant on the back. The sentence may also tell how or when to plant the seeds, suggest tools needed to do the planting, or remind the grower of foods what can be made from the harvested plant.

# WORD STAIRS

*Enhance the child's ability to build words, step by step.*

**WHAT YOU'LL NEED:** pencil, paper

Begin by having the child write one vocabulary word across the bottom of a piece of paper. Encourage the child to check the spelling of the word by looking up the word in dictionary, checking it on a computer spell checker, finding it in a book or magazine, or confirming the spelling with you or another adult.

Then to build the next step in the word stairs, the child must think of a word that ends with the same last letter as the first word. The new word should be written vertically on the paper as shown. The third word must begin with the same first letter as the second word and should be written across the page. Continue this process until a staircase of words has been created from the bottom to the top of the paper. Use a larger piece of paper and challenge the child see how high he or she can build a staircase.

# PLENTY OF PASTA

118... 119

*This clever approach to writing new sight words will have the child glued to the paper—literally.*

**WHAT YOU'LL NEED:** alphabet pasta, glue, heavy paper

Invite the child to use alphabet pasta to write new vocabulary words. Have the child select the necessary pasta letters and arrange them in order to spell the words. Help the child glue the letters on heavy paper. When the glue is dry, the child can trace the letters with his or her fingers and say the words. The child may use the new words in sentences, too.

# MISCHIEF MAKERS

*A little word mischief will add just the right amount of intrigue and excitement to vocabulary building.*

**WHAT YOU'LL NEED:** large index cards, markers, clear tape or sticky notes

Invite the child to make labels for different objects in the room, such as doors, cabinets, computers, and so on. Have the child tape the labels beside or on the corresponding objects. After a few days, secretly mix up some of the labels. Then tell the child that the labels have been moved by a mystery mischief maker, and encourage him or her to return them to their correct places.

## 121 WORD-A-DAY

*Learn new words every day of the week with this "drip dry" method.*

**WHAT YOU'LL NEED:** clothesline pouch (zipper bag, drawstring sack, or other container), large index cards, clothespins, clothesline, markers

String a clothesline across one corner of the room and set out a bag or box of clothespins. Next write interesting theme-related words on index cards. Choose words such as *caterpillar, cocoon,* and *butterfly* (from a science project) or *square, circle,* and *triangle* (from a math lesson on shapes). Place the words in the clothesline pouch.

Each day invite the child to pick a word from the pouch. Help the child say the word, use it in a sentence, and illustrate it when applicable. Then have the child clip the new word to the clothesline to review later.

## SILLY VERSES 122

*Nouns and verbs become the silly lyrics to new verses of "Row, Row, Row Your Boat."*

Display a copy of the song "Row, Row, Row Your Boat," pointing to the words as you sing the song together. Circle the words *row* and *boat.* Let the child think of pairs of verbs and nouns to replace the circled ones. Sing verses of the song using the words the child suggested. Some silly new verses might include:

Ride, ride, ride, your bike, gently down the stream . . .

Jump, jump, jump the lilypads, gently down the stream . . .

# ONE-SYLLABLE ALIEN

**123**

*An alien visits Earth to teach young Earthlings about one-syllable words.*

**WHAT YOU'LL NEED:** box or backpack, masking tape, cards, markers

Pretend that an alien lands its spacecraft at the child's school or home. It has come to collect objects to take back to a faraway planet. The alien, however, only collects objects that have one-syllable names. Invite the child to collect one-syllable objects for the alien, label them, and place them in a backpack or box for easy transporting. Then have the child make a list of one-syllable words for the alien to take back to its faraway planet. How many does the child know?

**124**

# ONE BY ONE

*How can you change a bug into a pup in six easy steps? Play this challenging word game and find out!*

bug
bag
rag
rat
pat
put
pup

**WHAT YOU'LL NEED:** paper, pencil

Write the word *bug* on a piece of paper. Now make a new word by changing one letter. Perhaps you will change the *u* to an *a* to make the word *bag*. Continue the game in this way to see how many new words the child makes before ending up with the word *pup*. For continued play, try using other words to start and finish with.

# SIMPLE AS A SIMILE

**125**

*As tall as a skyscraper or as strong as an ox, this simile activity is sure to be a big, big hit with children.*

**WHAT YOU'LL NEED:** bag, several small household objects, poetry collection

Have the child read poems that use *similes.* Point out the similes and explain that these phrases use the words *as* or *like* to compare two things. Next place several small objects in a bag. Let the child remove one object at a time from the bag and use a simile to describe or compare its size to another object. Use the following format to get the child thinking:

| |
|---|
| ___ is as big as ___ |
| ___ is as strong as ___ |
| ___ is as wide as ___ |
| ___ is as round as ___ |

# PHONICS FORTUNES

In this imaginative array of phonics activities, the child will learn, review, and practice basic phonics skills such as initial consonant sounds, short and long vowel sounds, prefixes and suffixes, *r*-controlled vowels, and much, much more. Whether playing Waste Paper Basketball, making a Phonics Salad, or building Ice Cream Syllables, the child will be sure to have fun with phonics!

## 126 LETTER COLLAGES

*Cut it, glue it, paste it! This creative activity is sure to keep busy hands interested in phonics.*

**WHAT YOU'LL NEED:** ABC books, heavy paper (precut into large letters), old magazines, clear tape or glue, blunt scissors, hole punch, string

Read aloud a variety of ABC books with the child. Point out the pictures, the letters, and the corresponding beginning sounds as you read. Next give the child large paper letters that you have cut out in advance. Ask the child to cut out pictures from old magazines of objects that begin with the sound each letter stands for—for example, a cat and a car for the letter *C,* and a dog, deer, and door for the letter *D.* Encourage the child to cover the entire letter with the pictures to create a colorful letter collage. To complete the project, punch a hole in the top of each letter and hang it in a room.

# MARK IT!

*The child will enjoy looking and reading with you while
learning about beginning sounds. Pull up a chair!*

**WHAT YOU'LL NEED:** sticky notes, picture book, pencil

Choose a favorite picture book with the child. Then have the child write one consonant on five separate sticky notes. While the child pages through the picture book, ask him or her to mark five objects or words in the book with the corresponding sticky note. Invite the child to share the book with you, pointing out the words and pictures the child has marked with the sticky notes.

# EXPRESS MAIL

*Writing, mailing, and delivering these special phonics
letters will keep the young mail carrier's hands full.*

**WHAT YOU'LL NEED:** 3 shoe boxes with lids, envelopes, crayons,
3×5-inch index cards, blunt scissors

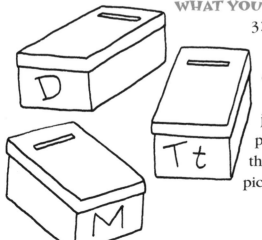

Cut a slit in the lid of each shoe box. Write a letter (or cluster of letters, such as *d, t, str,* or *m*) on the front of each box. Invite the child to pretend to be a mail carrier whose job is to sort and deliver the mail. Have the child draw pictures of objects on the index cards that begin with each of the letters on the mailboxes. Then have the child place each picture in an envelope and deliver them to the correct mailbox.

# SUFFIX BINGO

*This twist on the familiar board game is a motivating way to apply knowledge of word endings.*

Prepare and distribute bingo cards with nine-square grids. Have players randomly write the following word endings, or suffixes, in the grid boxes: *s, es, ed, ing, less, ly, ful, er,* and *est.* To play the game, say words that contain one of the suffixes. Then have players cover the appropriate suffix on their playing card. The first player to cover three suffixes in a row shouts "BINGO" and is declared the winner.

# TONGUE TWISTERS

*Try this tongue twister out, and see who gets tongue-tied first.*

Say the following tongue twister "Peter Piper" slowly to the child. Then invite the child to repeat it. Ask the child what he or she noticed about the words. Stir up some fun by having the child repeat the tongue twister over and over, saying it faster each time. Have the child name other things Peter could have picked that would begin with the same letter. Use the new words in the tongue twister.

Peter Piper picked a peck of pickled peppers;

A peck of pickled peppers Peter Piper picked.

If Peter Piper picked a peck of pickled peppers,

Where's the peck of pickled peppers Peter Piper picked?

# DEAR WISE OWL

*Invite the child to solve this mini-mystery about a mysterious box.*

**WHAT YOU'LL NEED:** large piece of construction paper, markers, notebook paper, pencil

Read the following letter to the child:

> Dear Wise Owl,
>
>   When I opened the front door this morning, there was a large box on my doorstep. It was wrapped in shiny red paper and had a giant bow. Just as I was about to open the box, it moved! What do you think is in the box? What should I do with it?
>
>   Please tell me what you think!
>
> Brandon

Have the child write the letters of the alphabet down the left side of a large piece of construction paper. Ask him or her to suggest creative ideas for what may be in the box. Invite the child to think of a word that begins with each letter, or as many of the letters as he or she can, and write them on a sheet of paper. Have the child decide on one item from the list that he or she thinks is most likely in the box. Then help the child write a response to Brandon, telling him what the child thinks is in the box and what he or she thinks Brandon should do about it.

# SPORTSWRITERS

132

*In every sporting event, sportwriters need to be there to get the story. So grab your pencil!*

**WHAT YOU'LL NEED:** old newspapers, blunt scissors, paper, pencils, clear tape or glue

Invite the child to pretend to be a sportswriter. Page through the sports section of a newspaper to familiarize the child with headlines, photo captions, and stories. Then help the child collect the tools for the next assignment, including a pencil or two, paper, and some newspapers. Explain that his or her task is to capture, in a single sentence, the main idea or most important moment of a sporting event. Explain how important this story is and how it will appear on the front page of tomorrow's sports section in the local newspaper.

First have the young sportswriter cut out a picture of someone participating in a sport. Invite the child to write a caption or headline, such as the one pictured here, about the athlete using as many words as possible with a particular phonics sound, such as long *o*. Glue or tape the headline on newsprint to resemble a newspaper.

133

# SIMON SAYS

*Simon Says that children and adults alike will love this silly version of the popular game.*

Remind players of the rules for Simon Says. Explain that you will play the game as it is normally played, with the following exception: The players should only follow a command if it begins with a *w* (or another target letter). For example, players can walk, wave, waddle, and wiggle but never hop, clap, or sing.

# BAG IT!

**134**

*The child will "Bag It!" while learning about vowel sounds.*

**WHAT YOU'LL NEED:** 5 paper bags with handles, small common household items

Write the vowels—*a, e, i, o,* and *u*—on each bag as shown. Find a small household item with a vowel sound in its name and place it inside the corresponding bag. Then place the bag on the back of a child's chair. Invite the child to find another item with the same vowel sound and place it in the corresponding bag. Now it's your turn to find an item with a different vowel sound and place it inside the corresponding bag. Continue taking turns placing items in the bags until all vowel sounds have been used.

**135**

# SING-ALONG #2

*The child will enjoy singing along with this new version of a familiar song while practicing initial consonant sounds.*

Focus on a particular letter or a cluster of letters together, such as *cl, gr,* or *sch.* Help the child suggest words that begin with the chosen letter or letters. Then sing the following phonics song to the tune of "Did You Ever See a Lassie?" together, using the suggested words. For example:

Did you ever hear a (t) word, a (t) word, a (t) word? Did you ever hear a (t)word, a (t) word like ___turtle___ ?

# CORNER-TO-CORNER PUZZLE

*This twist to the crossword puzzle helps the child practice words containing r-controlled vowels.*

**WHAT YOU'LL NEED:** paper, pencil

Draw a corner-to-corner puzzle on paper like the one shown here. Explain the following phonics rule pertaining to vowels followed by *r: ar* stands for the sound you hear in *star; or* stands for the sound you hear in *horse; ir, ur,* and *er* stand for the sounds you hear in *skirt, nurse,* and *fern.* After reviewing the sounds, give picture or word clues for each *r*-controlled vowel and let the child complete the puzzle.

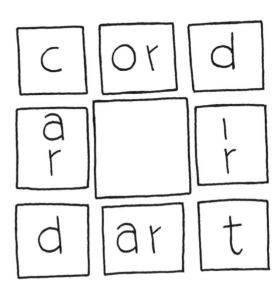

## ACTIVITY TWIST

Invite the child to make up his or her own corner-to-corner puzzle and challenge you to fill it out.

## 137 SYLLA-BALL

*The child will roll with laughter while playing this build-a-syllable, word-making game.*

**WHAT YOU'LL NEED:** softball

Begin the game by sitting on the floor facing each other. Start by saying the first syllable of a familiar word, such as *mon,* while rolling the ball to the child. Once the child catches the ball, he or she must repeat the first syllable and quickly add the second syllable, such *ster,* to make *monster.* If the child finishes the word, one point is given. Play continues until the child reaches ten points.

## VESTED INTEREST 138

*The child will have a vested interest in beginning letters and sounds while designing decorative vests.*

**WHAT YOU'LL NEED:** paper bag, blunt scissors, paint, paintbrushes, old magazines

Cut a large paper bag straight up the middle. Make a neck opening by cutting an oval shape in the top of the bag. Make arm holes by cutting circles in the sides of the bag. Invite the child to decorate the newly created vest by painting letters on the vest and adding pictures from old magazines of objects that begin with that letter.

# RIDDLE GAME

· · · · · · · · · · · · · · · · · · · · · · **139**

*Share jokes and riddles with the child in this
rib-tickling activity about letter sounds.*

Tell the child that you are going to ask for an answer to a riddle. Explain that there may be more than one answer to the question, or riddle, but the correct answer must have a designated long vowel sound either in the middle or at the end of the word. See the following examples:

Long *e*—What insect makes honey in its hive? (bee)

Long *e*—Which bee rules the worker bees? (queen)

**140**

# PUDDING PLAY

▬ ▬ ▬ ▬ ▬ ▬ ▬ ▬ ▬ ▬ ▬ ▬ ▬ ▬

*Finger painting was never so much fun as it is with this
pudding project. And cleanup is as easy as 1–2–3!*

**WHAT YOU'LL NEED:** premixed pudding, sponge, dish pan filled with soapy water, clean work surface

Begin by pouring a cup of pudding on a clean, flat working surface. Invite the child to spread it around with his or her fingers. Then review final consonants by saying a word and having the child write the whole word or just the final letter in the pudding. The child can erase his or her work by rubbing over it with fingertips. Continue by having the child write and erase final consonants for as long as the pudding lasts. Pudding inevitably gets licked off fingers and out of the bowl during this activity, so it will not last too long. For easy cleanup, set out the soapy water and sponge.

# PHONICS SALAD

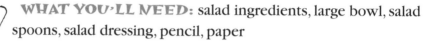

*Toss some phonics in your recipe for a healthy, educational salad!*

**WHAT YOU'LL NEED:** salad ingredients, large bowl, salad spoons, salad dressing, pencil, paper

Explain to the child that there are all sorts of salads, including vegetable salad, fruit salad, and salad with meat or pasta. Begin by listing all of the ingredients you can put into a salad. Next make a real salad using only ingredients that have a short vowel sound. For example, suggest a tossed vegetable salad that could have any or all of the following short vowel ingredients: lettuce, radish, celery, mushroom, egg, asparagus, olive, ham, bell pepper, and others. Top the salad with a favorite dressing and enjoy the finished product! (If you do not want to make a real salad, you can easily adapt this activity to writing the ingredients on a recipe card.)

# LONG VOWEL HUNT

*In the cupboard? In the toy box? Who knows where the child will find objects needed for this vowel hunt.*

**WHAT YOU'LL NEED:** construction paper, markers

Fold a large piece of paper into five columns. Write these headings at the top: Long A, Long E, Long I, Long O, Long U. Review these sounds together. Next have the child walk around the room (house, yard) in search of objects that contain one of the vowel sounds. Ask the child to find at least three objects for each long vowel. Have the child write the name of each object found in the appropriate column on the paper.

## 143 RUB-A-DUB-DUB

▼▼▼▼▼▼▼▼▼▼▼▼▼▼▼▼▼▼▼▼▼▼▼▼▼▼▼▼▼▼

*Invite the child to rub-a-dub-dub objects with a specific sound to make an attractive piece of art.*

**WHAT YOU'LL NEED:** newsprint, pencil, paper bag or cardboard box

Take a nature walk with the child. Bring along a collection bag or box, newsprint, and a pencil. While walking, ask the child to look for objects that have a target sound, such as long *e.* The child should then place each object in the collection bag until he or she has at least five things. Help the child arrange the objects on a flat, hard surface. Then cover the collection with newsprint and invite the child to rub over the top carefully with a pencil. The result will be an interesting print. Invite the child to complete the print by labeling each object on the paper. You may wish to mat the prints and display them in a prominent place.

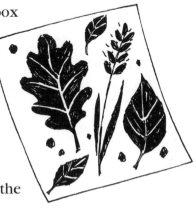

## WASTEPAPER BASKETBALL 144

▬ ▬ ▬ ▬ ▬ ▬ ▬ ▬ ▬ ▬ ▬ ▬

*The child will enjoy hooping it up with this mock basketball activity!*

**WHAT YOU'LL NEED:** old magazines, blunt scissors, wastebasket

Mark the floor at two distances from the wastebasket, for example four to five feet and seven to eight feet. Invite the child to choose a digraph. Explain that a digraph is two letters that form one sound, such as *sh* or *th.* Next have the child cut out pictures from old magazines with objects that begin or end with the target sound. Crumple each picture that *begins* with the sound and place it at the closest line. Crumple each picture that *ends* with the sound and place it at the *farthest* line. The child tosses each piece of wadded paper from the appropriate line, trying to make a basket: one point is scored for short shots and two points for long shots.

# STAR MOBILE

**145**

▼▼▼▼▼▼▼▼▼▼▼▼▼▼▼▼▼▼▼▼▼▼▼▼▼▼▼▼▼▼

*Star light, star bright, the first star the child sees tonight will be from this attractive vowel mobile.*

**WHAT YOU'LL NEED:** sturdy paper, blunt scissors, aluminum foil, markers, heavy string, clear tape, masking tape

Cut a piece of sturdy paper into a large star shape, cover it with aluminum foil, and write the word *star* on it. Then cut several small star shapes, covering each with aluminum foil. Next invite the child to find other examples of words with the letter pattern *ar* and have him or her write each word on a piece of masking tape, and attach to the smaller star shapes—one word per star. Tape pieces of heavy string to the top of each small star. Complete the mobile by taping the smaller stars to the larger one as shown.

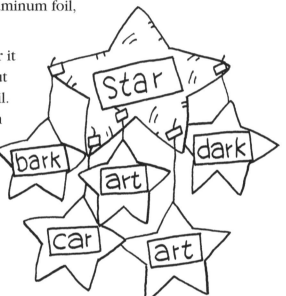

# ACTIVITY TWIST

Invite the child to make other mobiles using star shapes and words that contain the following letter patterns:

| | | | |
|---|---|---|---|
| bird | *ir* | horse | *or* |
| letter | *er* | purse | *ur* |

# SYLLABLE BUGS

**146**

*Creepy, slimy, itchy bugs have invaded
this syllable activity. Watch out!*

**WHAT YOU'LL NEED:** egg carton cups, pipe cleaner pieces, blunt scissors

Make insect models with egg carton cups. First separate the egg cups by cutting an egg carton apart. Next ask the child to think of an insect, perhaps a butterfly or a caterpillar. Help the child determine how many syllables are in the word. Then have the child write each syllable in the insect's name on an egg cup, one syllable per cup.

Then use short pieces of pipe cleaners to attach the cups together. Bend and twist additional pipe cleaners, poking them through the cups, to create antennae, wings, or other features that you and the child would like to add to make the insect look complete (see illustration). For continued syllabic fun, choose from these other insects: beetle, bumblebee, hornet, centipede, and grasshopper.

# HOP, HOP-A-RALLY

**147**

*The child can hop to rhyming success with
this interactive hopping activity.*

See how many times the child can hop on one foot while practicing rhyming. Begin by chanting this rhyme: Chickety, chickety, chop. How long before I stop?

After you finish the chant, ask the child to name words that rhyme with chop and stop. Have the child hop once for each rhyming word. How long can he or she hop?

## 148 KNOCK, KNOCK, NONSENSE

*Explore consonant sounds while sharing favorite knock-knock jokes.*

Teach the child the formula for knock-knock jokes while sharing some of your favorites. Then invite the child to make up knock-knock jokes using words spelled with the consonant digraphs *sh, ch, wh, th, ph,* and *gh.* You may wish to start with the cheetah and gopher jokes shown here. But be warned: Telling knock-knock jokes is contagious.

Knock, Knock, who's there? Cheetah. Cheetah who? A cheetah never wins.

Knock, Knock, who's there? Gopher. Gopher who? Gopher a want to gopher a hamburger?

## STRANGE STRIPES 149

*Have you ever seen a striped strawberry? In this "strange" art activity, anything is possible.*

**WHAT YOU'LL NEED:** corrugated cardboard, large sheet of white construction paper, poster paints, paintbrush, blunt scissors

Review words with the consonant cluster *str* as in *stripe, strawberry,* and *street.* Then set out corrugated cardboard and blunt scissors and cut out a large strawberry. Invite the child to paint the corrugated side of the cutout. Then turn the wet cutout over and press it against a piece of white paper. The result is the print of a striped strawberry. Encourage the child to label the artwork.

# JOHNNY'S HAMMER

150

*Hammer away at syllable identification while singing.*

Chant the first verse of the following rhyme, "Johnny's Hammer," with the child. At the end of the first verse, have the child name a word with one syllable. Then chant the second verse together. This time the child must name a word with two syllables. Continue in this manner for verse three.

Johnny builds one hammer, one hammer, one hammer. Johnny builds one hammer all the day long.

Johnny builds two hammers, two hammers, two hammers. Johnny builds two hammers all the day long.

Johnny builds three hammers, three hammers, three hammers. Johnny builds three hammers all the day long.

151

# MARSHMALLOW MODELS

*Marshmallow models are a creative way to learn about letter sounds. And clean up is a cinch!*

**WHAT YOU'LL NEED:** large marshmallows, toothpicks, pencil, paper

Help the child list objects that begin with a targeted sound, perhaps those created with a silent letter, such as *kn* or *wr.* The objects might include knights, a wrench, or some other object of interest. Then set out marshmallows and toothpicks. Demonstrate how to connect marshmallows with toothpicks before inviting the child to help build models of the objects. Follow up by having the child write about his or her marshmallow model while eating some of the remaining marshmallows.

# ICE CREAM SYLLABLES

**152**

*Scoop up a triple-decker treat when you make your own ice cream syllables.*

**WHAT YOU'LL NEED:** blunt scissors, construction paper, glue or tape

Cut out triangle-shaped cones and ice cream scoops from construction paper. Write root words (such as *end, cap,* and *vent*), prefixes (such as *un* or *pre),* which go before a root word, and suffixes (such as *ed* or *ing),* which go after a root word on the scoops.

Next set out a large piece of construction paper and glue or tape the cones onto the paper. Then invite the child to make triple-decker syllable treats by combining the scoops and gluing or taping them on top of the paper ice cream cone to make a word. Challenge the child to see if he or she can use the word in a sentence.

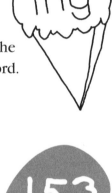

# FUNNY BONE TICKLE

**153**

*This game is sure to tickle your funny bone as actors do their silliest dramatizations of common words.*

**WHAT YOU'LL NEED:** paper, markers

Begin by making a list of homographs. Homographs are words that are spelled the same but have different meanings. You may wish to begin with the following examples and then add your own: *batter, ring, plant, brush.*

Here's how to play: One player chooses a word from the list. Then he or she tries to make the other players laugh by pantomiming one definition of the word, using impersonations and funny gestures. The first player who guesses the word gets to choose the next word.

# WRITING ROUNDUPS

Learning the fundamental skills of writing can be an enjoyable and creative experience for the child. With your guidance, the following assortment of activities—ranging from writing in cornmeal and making Top Ten lists to creating poems and journals—will open up an exciting world of writing to the young learner. And even though the activities are labeled by their level of difficulty, *all* activities are on the same level of fun. Be ready to adapt and change them, using whatever resources you have available to you. Many activities can be enhanced by adding illustrations. Be creative!

## SPLASH YOURSELF!

*Writing down descriptive words about oneself is a fun and creative way to learn about who you are!*

**WHAT YOU'LL NEED:** pencil, markers or crayons, paper, old magazines (optional)

Begin this activity by having the child brainstorm descriptive words about who he or she is—such as smart, kind, and fun—and write them on a piece of paper. This can be extended to include words or pictures cut out from magazines. Next have the child write his or her name in the center of a piece of paper. Have the child use markers or crayons to create a "splash" of words or pictures that describe him or herself. The child can then use the words to make descriptive sentences.

## 155 MY FAVORITE YEAR

*Every adult has a favorite year when many special events occur. This activity will preserve those memories.*

**WHAT YOU'LL NEED:** tape recorder, paper, pencil

Help the child prepare to interview an adult about a favorite year. Explain to the child how the following interviewing procedures are essential for a good interview: introducing oneself, having a list of good questions, allowing the adult to give complete answers, and thanking the adult when the interview is finished. Suggest the child follow the five W's used in newspaper reporting when he or she is planning the questions: who, what, when, where, and why.

After the interview is over, the child can listen to the tape and write down the favorite memories. Help the child create a small book or a birthday card that lists the highlights of the year. Save the tape for a permanent memory of the person interviewed.

## WORD WALK 156

*Use the great outdoors to encourage good listening and the writing of words associated with all the sounds you hear.*

**WHAT YOU'LL NEED:** clipboard, paper, pencil

Take a walk in your neighborhood. Have the child listen carefully to all the sounds heard. Write down the sounds. Some may have no regular spelling. In that case, have the child try to make up a spelling that seems logical, such as "zwee" for a whistle or "fawish" for a breeze. Explain that sometimes these made-up words become real words (this is called *onomatopoeia,* which means the spelling of the word is based on the vocal imitation of it).

# ACROSTIC POETRY

*This easy form of poetry can be used whenever a special day, person, or event calls for a poem.*

**WHAT YOU'LL NEED:** paper, markers

Perhaps it is Father's Day and the child needs to make a card. Suppose a special friend or family member needs a comforting thought. To create an acrostic poem, have the child write a key word, such as *father,* vertically on the left side of the paper. Then on each line, write a related word that begins with each letter, creating a poem such as the following:

**F**un

**A**lways helping

**T**errific

**H**ardworking

**E**xciting

**R**eady

For variety, the child can use two or more words for each line, creating a series of phrases.

# LOOPING INTO WRITING

## 158

*Looping helps get the brain working and provides a fundamental process for focusing on an idea.*

**WHAT YOU'LL NEED:** paper, pencil

Begin by inviting the child to do three minutes of freewriting, which means writing any words or phrases that come to mind. Encourage the child to write the entire time. Tell her or him not to worry about the quality of the writing, punctuation, and so on. When the designated time is up, have the child reread the work and circle one good idea. Then encourage the child to write on that idea for two to three minutes. Again, when the designated time is up, have the child reread the work and circle one good idea. You may need to repeat this process one more time.

When finished, the child will be ready to begin writing on the topic and be happy with the starting point. Encourage the child to use this process as a writing technique, and you'll be developing a writer!

## 159

# JOKING AROUND

*Consider "the source" when you need some laughter to liven up your day!*

**WHAT YOU'LL NEED:** stapler, paper, joke books (optional), pencil

Staple several pieces of paper together to make a book. Have the child write jokes you have heard in the book. Go to the library, and check out some joke books. Then have the child write favorite jokes found in the joke book. The child can also try creating original jokes or revising existing jokes to add to the collection. Share with friends and families, and have a constant source of laughter.

# LISTS, LISTS, LISTS!

**160**

*Involve the child in writing a regular household task, such as making a grocery list.*

**WHAT YOU'LL NEED:** grocery advertisements, blunt scissors, 3×5 index cards, clear tape or glue, pen or pencil

Collect a variety of colorful grocery advertisements that includes pictures and words. Have the child cut out the pictures of the grocery items you regularly purchase. Next the child should glue or tape the pictures to the back of index cards—one picture per card. Have the child write the word for each item on the front of the card. Then invite the child to make up a grocery list by copying the words from the front of the cards.

Once the words have been learned, have the child recall the correct spelling and write the words again using only the pictures. Just for fun, invite the child to make grocery lists for storybook characters, such as Mama Bear's list from *The Three Bears* or Little Red Riding Hood's list. Don't forget lists for special occasions, such as birthdays, holidays, picnics, and so on.

# PALINDROME FUN

**161**

*In this activity, the child will practice letter recognition while learning about palindromes.*

**WHAT YOU'LL NEED:** paper, pencil

Palindromes are words that can be read the same forward and backward: mom, pop, dad, noon, pup, gag, level, tot. Discuss some examples with the child. Then think of more words and have the child write them in a notebook. Check with the library for books that give examples of palindromes and explore those with the child. Extend the activity by inviting the child to add illustrations.

## 162 — MY BODY AND ME

*Combine art and writing while the child learns his or her body size and parts.*

**WHAT YOU'LL NEED:** butcher paper, pencil, blunt scissors, sticky notes

Begin by placing a large piece of butcher paper on the floor. The paper should be big enough for the child to lay on. Then take a pencil and draw around the child. Next use scissors to cut out the outline carefully. Have the child write names of body parts on sticky notes, then place the notes on the appropriate parts of the body.

Vary this activity by having the child lay on the paper in amusing poses, such as a weight lifter. Have the child draw the barbells and add it to the drawing. Another variation includes adding clothes for different types of weather, such as a pair of pants, coat, or hat. Lay the clothing on the paper, following the same outlining process, and have the child label the clothing. "Dress" the body parts when planning how to get ready for a rainy, sunny, or snowy day.

## VERSES AND MORE VERSES — 163

*You don't have to be a trained singer to have fun with this singing and writing activity.*

**WHAT YOU'LL NEED:** paper, pencil

Sing a favorite song together such as "Hush Little Baby," "Eensy Weensy Spider," or "I Know an Old Woman Who Swallowed a Fly." Show and explain how new verses are sometimes written just for fun to be shared with others. Explain how most simple songs rhyme and discuss what a rhyme is. Then try creating some new verses, singing them together. Have the child write the new verses on a piece of paper. Encourage the child to share with others, inviting them to add verses to the song, too.

## **164** "I REMEMBER" POEM

*This activity is perfect for sharing an unforgettable memory with a favorite relative or friend.*

**WHAT YOU'LL NEED:** paper, pencil or markers

When a special occasion is approaching, such as a birthday, Mother's Day, or Father's Day, have the child think of all the memories related to time shared with that person. Invite the child to write down a word or two about each memory. Then have the child create a series of sentences. Most of the sentences should begin with "I remember. . ." Arrange in a poem.

I remember when I loved to read in my dad's office.

I remember that there was just enough room between his bookshelves for me to curl up.

I remember that it was always quiet there.

But most of all

I remember that the heater kept me warm!

## LEGACY **165**

*Passing a legacy on to a friend or sibling can be a memorable and loving gift.*

**WHAT YOU'LL NEED:** paper, pencil

Explain to the child that a legacy is something that is passed on from person to person. It need not be money but could be a favorite book, a beloved toy, or something that you had painted, drawn, or written. At an appropriate time (birthday or New Year's Eve) have the child create a legacy for a sibling or friend. Share the legacy with the recipient.

# FAIRY TALE SPIN

166

*Did the wolf in The Three Little Pigs get a fair deal?*
*This activity lets other fairy tale characters be heard.*

**WHAT YOU'LL NEED:** fairy tale, such as *The Three Little Pigs;* paper; pencil

Read or tell a familiar fairy tale to the child. Good examples include *The Three Little Pigs,* *Cinderella, Little Red Riding Hood,* and *Jack and the Beanstalk.* After sharing the fairy tale, talk about how sometimes people are misunderstood. Relate the stories to misunderstandings the child may have experienced, perhaps a disagreement with a sibling or friend. Discuss how the fairy tale characters who seemed bad maybe didn't mean to be bad. For example, perhaps the wolf in *The Three Little Pigs* just wanted to be friends with the pigs.

After thinking of a lot of possibilities for new ways of looking at a story from a different character's point of view, have the child write a new story spinning off from the old story.

167

# BEGINNING JOURNAL

*Keeping a journal is a creative way to document events.*
*Try this easy journal for the beginning writer.*

**WHAT YOU'LL NEED:** notebook, pencil or markers

Begin by inviting the child to draw pictures of things that happened during the day. Then have the child add a few key words under the pictures so the events are remembered. Be sure each entry is dated. As the child's writing skills improve, help the child create complete sentences. You can also add a sentence or two each day as well. Turn this into a creative end-of-the-day activity.

**168** — **SIMILE POEMS**

*Once the child understands similes, they become easier to create!*

**WHAT YOU'LL NEED:** paper, pencil, examples of similes from poetry books for young children

This form of poetry is perfect for honoring a family member, creating a special card, or delighting a friend. The simile poem uses several sentences that have similes, which are two unlike thoughts that are compared to each other. The key words that identify a simile are *like* and *as.* The poem can be as short as two lines, such as the following examples, or as long as the young poet prefers. For an extension, have the child consider making a "simile book" and keep favorites that are heard or read for use in later writings.

Mother is **like** a soft pillow
Her lap is as soft **as** a cloud.

My cat is **like** a ball of fur.
Her paws are as soft **as** velvet.

**FOOD RIDDLE** **169**

*Describing food characteristics will enhance the child's descriptive vocabulary—and make your mouth water!*

**WHAT YOU'LL NEED:** foods that have distinctive characteristics (orange, apple, banana, squash, and so on), paper, pencil

Have the child choose a food and make a list of all its characteristics without telling what the food is. For example, suggest that the list for an orange include words such as *bumpy, round, skin, sweet,* and so on. Invite the child to try to stump you by reading all the characteristics of a particular food without telling its name.

**170**

# TAKING A MESSAGE

*Taking a phone message is an important skill and can be taught using this fairy tale activity.*

**WHAT YOU'LL NEED:** pink message forms or notepaper, fairy tales, pencil

Read a favorite fairy tale, such as *Little Red Riding Hood*, aloud with the child. Discuss what Little Red might have said if she had phoned home when the wolf was about to eat her: "Mom! Call the woodsman! Grandmother is too hairy!" What message would the three bears have left with the police if Goldilocks hadn't run away? Have the child write the message on the pink pad or notepaper.

## ACTIVITY TWIST

Brainstorm with the child about what Little Red's mother might have said after she received the message about grandmother? Invite the child to write a new story ending.

# SENSE-A-TIONAL POEM

*This irresistible form of poetry helps budding
poets understand the body's senses.*

**WHAT YOU'LL NEED:** paper, pencil

Introduce the body's five senses: tasting, hearing, smelling, seeing, and touching. Talk about how each of these senses help the child appreciate the world. Think of a topic or idea that could be described by the senses, such as food, a season, or an event (carnival, birthday, holiday). Share the example of the poem's format below. Then share the example poem. Have the child create a poem using the same format.

**Line 1:** color of topic or idea

Winter wears white and gray.

**Line 2:** tastes like

It tastes like ice on the tongue.

**Line 3:** sounds like

It sounds like whispers in the night,

**Line 4:** smells like

Yet it smells cool and clear.

**Line 5:** looks like

It looks like fairyland in the dark,

**Line 6:** feels like

And sends shivers to all who feel its chill.

## 172  GOING TO THE ZOO

*You can create an exciting zoo and help your child's writing at the same time with this activity.*

**WHAT YOU'LL NEED:** stuffed animals, 3×5-inch index cards, boxes for cages, clear tape, pencil or markers, blunt scissors

Help the child collect a variety of stuffed animals. Then have the child write each animal's name on an index card. Next take the empty boxes and cut out a window in each box. Place each animal in a box and have the child tape the card with the animal's name under the window.

For a more challenging activity, have the child include background information about the animal. Extend this activity by writing directions for visitors, creating a "map" of the zoo with a list of the animals they will see.

## EMBARRASSING MOMENTS  173

*Everyone has a memory that brings back a red face or a chuckle. Use that to inspire some great writing.*

**WHAT YOU'LL NEED:** paper, pencil

Begin by sharing an embarrassing or scary experience you had with the child. Perhaps you went to school with two different socks on. Maybe the teacher caught you not paying attention in class because you were talking to a friend. Talk about embarrassing things that the child has experienced. Then have the child write about the event, making it as humorous as possible.

# FAMILY NEWSLETTER

*Start a new family tradition that benefits everyone, especially if family members live far apart.*

**WHAT YOU'LL NEED:** pencil, paper, envelope, postage stamp

Invite the child to create a newsletter that has one or more short articles about family events. The newsletter can be as simple as one page written in pencil or as elaborate as something done on a computer, complete with special fonts and art. Then have the child send the newsletter to a relative along with a list of other relatives' addresses and the route the newsletter should take. A note asking all recipients to add their news to the newsletter also should be enclosed.

When it arrives back to the child, he or she should replace the information that has circulated with new information. Then have the child send it off again, following the same route as the first edition of the newsletter, instructing family members to replace circulated information with new information. This way everyone gets the latest family news without having to write individual letters to family members.

## 175 AWAY WE GO

*Making a travel brochure will get anyone in the mood to travel!*

**WHAT YOU'LL NEED:** paper, markers, pictures (optional)

This activity can be used to plan a trip or to serve as a record of a vacation. If creating the brochure before a trip, use the library to gather information about the destination. You can also go to a travel agency and pick up some sample brochures. Then help the child create a brochure that convinces someone else that the destination chosen for the brochure is the ideal vacation spot.

If you want to do this activity after you've been to a particular place, collect information while on the trip. Invite the child to create the brochure by using postcards or photographs collected on the trip.

## WRAPPING IT UP 176

*Instead of buying expensive wrapping paper, try this creative way of sharing one's writing.*

**WHAT YOU'LL NEED:** paper, markers, ribbon

Think of related words for a particular holiday together where gift-giving is involved. For example, you may list *caring, cook, career woman,* and *cheerful* for Mother's Day. Plan how these words can make a pleasing pattern on paper. Perhaps each word has its own color or a special shape. Work carefully on paper so that the words are not smudged as the child writes them. Then use the paper and some ribbon to wrap a gift.

# TALL TALES #2

**177**

*Sometimes it's fun to exaggerate—the bigger the better!*
*This activity helps develop a young writer's imagination.*

**WHAT YOU'LL NEED:** paper, pencil, and tall tales (optional)

Many tall tales, such as those about Pecos Bill or Paul Bunyan, are built on the theme of settling the West in America. They also rely on exaggeration, or *hyperbole.* For example, the horse Widow-Maker could buck as high as the moon.

Read some tall tales together that contain a lot of pictures. Discuss exaggeration and give examples, such as "I'm so hungry I could eat a horse" and "It's so hot I'm melting." Invite the child to make up and write down other examples. This can be kept in a book of writing ideas that can later be incorporated into other writing.

**178**

# INTERACTIVE JOURNAL

*Share daily events by writing notes to each*
*other in this interactive journal.*

**WHAT YOU'LL NEED:** notebook, pencils

Explain that in this journal you and the child will both be writing notes or letters to each other, describing daily events and asking interesting questions. For the beginning writer, encourage the child to draw pictures when he or she does not know how to spell a word. Begin the journal by sharing details about your day. End your entry by asking questions about the child's day. Invite the child to do the same, and continue alternating entries.

To vary the writing, colored pencils can be used, or the activity can take on a particular form, such as an acrostic poem (see page 101) or a simile poem (see page 107).

## 179 TOP TEN LIST

*Making lists is a popular and fun way to motivate a reluctant writer.*

**WHAT YOU'LL NEED:** paper, pencil

Invite the child to create a list of top ten all-time favorite things to do, such as staying in bed. Then he or she can create a list of reasons to do the opposite, such as in these examples.

### TEN REASONS TO STAY IN BED

It's a school day.

I haven't studied for spelling.

My toe hurts.

My turtle will be lonely if I go.

My friend is sick.

It's meat loaf day at school.

My pinkie hurts.

My dog will be lonely if I go.

It's raining outside.

I want to watch television.

### TEN REASONS TO GET OUT OF BED

It's a school day.

I need to study for spelling.

Mom will tell me to wash dishes if I stay home.

My turtle wants to hibernate.

My friend is coming over.

It's brownie day at school.

Dad will tell me to clean the house if I stay home.

My dog just wants to sleep anyway.

I can go out and see a rainbow.

Mom unplugged the television.

## ACTIVITY TWIST

While the child writes one version of a top ten list, write your own amusing list of reasons why you should or should not stay in bed. Compare lists for added enjoyment.

# ON THE GO

**180**

▼▼▼▼▼▼▼▼▼▼▼▼▼▼▼▼▼▼▼▼▼▼▼▼▼▼▼

*Use those spare moments in the car to keep the child reading and writing (and busy!).*

**WHAT YOU'LL NEED:** clipboard, paper, pencil

The child can see a lot of words—on signs, billboards, in store windows—as you go on errands, take short trips, or travel to and from school. Keep a clipboard, paper, and pencil in the car. As you travel, have the child copy the names of the stores you frequently go to. Keep the list and invite the child to practice reading and writing the names. Once the child is familiar with the names, have the child list the places in the order that you will go. For more challenging directions, add street names to the list.

# STORY PLAY

**181**

● ● ● ● ● ● ● ● ● ● ● ● ● ● ● ● ● ● ● ● ● ● ● ●

*Stuffed animals and simple stories combine perfectly to give the child an opportunity to develop simple scripts.*

**WHAT YOU'LL NEED:** stuffed animals, simple story, paper, pencil

Collect a variety of stuffed animals. Then share a simple story with the child. Discuss how the story can be acted out with the stuffed animals. Make a list of characters together and plan which animal will play what character. Then help the child write the story into script form. Read the script aloud while the animals act out the story. Revise the script as necessary after the first rehearsal. Prepare the play and share with others.

# MUSICAL WORDS

## 182

*Combine writing with music for this inspirational activity.*

**WHAT YOU'LL NEED:** recording of theme-related music (such as scary, water, or cowboy), pencil, paper

Choose a place where the child will not be disturbed. Explain that you will be playing some music that should make the child think of related words. For the beginning writer, you may want to tell the child what kind of music you will play. For the older child, let him or her try to determine what kind of music it is.

Invite the child to listen to the music and write down all the words the music prompts. As the music continues, the child may want to take a second piece of paper and arrange the words in a new design that combines the words with an illustration. For example, water music may prompt a drawing of the ocean with words on waves.

# SLEEPY TIME RECIPE

**183**

*Getting ready for bed can be a sweet experience
with this writing and sharing activity.*

**WHAT YOU'LL NEED:** paper, pencil

Discuss with the child the interesting things that happen at night. For example the stars come out, the fairies put stardust in the child's eyes, and the moon comes up. Talk about recipes and how ingredients can carefully be mixed to make a special treat. Have the child make a list of all the ingredients that would be perfect for a good night's sleep. Then invite the child to create a "recipe," deciding what amounts would be just right. For example, a child may want two cups of stardust to dust the whole room; maybe even just a pinch for the eyes. Is the whole moon necessary or just a slice?

After the child has written the recipe, have the child read it at bedtime. For a variation, make a wake-up recipe using the same process.

**184**

# WHERE WOULD I LIVE?

*Learning how to compare features of different places can
be a useful skill. Start by comparing city and country.*

**WHAT YOU'LL NEED:** paper, pencil

Have the child make a chart by writing CITY on one side of the paper and COUNTRY on the other side. Then have the child list the features of each area. Once the features have been listed, discuss the advantages and disadvantages of both areas. Follow the example on the right.

| COUNTRY | CITY |
|---------|------|
| Quiet | Exciting |
| Fields | Streets |
| Trees | Buildings |

## 185 LIGHTS OUT STORIES

▼▼▼▼▼▼▼▼▼▼▼▼▼▼▼▼▼▼▼▼▼▼▼▼▼▼

*Just what happens in the house when the lights go out at night? Perhaps it isn't what we think!*

**WHAT YOU'LL NEED:** paper, pencil

We all know that sometimes toys appear to come alive and take on their own personalities. But what about those plain, ordinary items we find in other parts of the house? Have the child think about all the various items stored in the kitchen: blender, mixer, spoons, spices, coffee maker, toaster, and so on. Would the knives be mean and the spoons be sweet? Would the bigger items try to control the little ones? Would they all get out and make special foods for the pets?

Think about different possibilities. Then invite the child to write a highly imaginative story about what really happens during those magical hours.

# PBJ Fun

**186**

*Warning! This is only for brave adults! Be prepared to be messy!*

**WHAT YOU'LL NEED:** paper, pencil, bread, peanut butter, jelly, butter knife, plate

Everyone thinks they know how to write good directions. After all, how hard could it be to write directions for something as simple as creating a peanut butter and jelly sandwich?

In this activity, invite the child to write the directions for making this favorite sandwich. Then you must follow the steps exactly as written. For example, if Step 1 says "Spread the peanut butter on the bread," you will have to use your fingers for spreading the peanut butter. Nothing was said about using a knife! After the sandwich has been made, discuss the importance of detailed instructions. Have the child rewrite the directions and try again. *Bon appétit!*

**187** # Corny Writing

*Instead of sand, invite the child to write in cornmeal!*

**WHAT YOU'LL NEED:** plastic dishpan or other container, enough cornmeal to provide about a 1-inch-deep layer in dishpan

Place the cornmeal in the bottom of the container. Have the child smooth it out with his or her hand. Suggest words for the child to write in the cornmeal, or the child can practice writing words alone. The texture feels great and the child will enjoy this kind of writing. Cover the cornmeal or return it to a glass jar when finished.

# TREE OF WORDS

*Try this activity when trees are colorful in the fall or when they are just beginning to sprout new leaves in the spring.*

**WHAT YOU'LL NEED:** large piece of paper, pencils, crayons, notebook

Begin by taking a walk with the child, talking about the trees in the neighborhood. Take along paper and pencil and have the child write down all the "tree" words used, such as *branch, leaves,* or *trunk.* Next draw a big tree on a large piece of paper, including branches and leaves. Then invite the child to write the tree words in their correct location on the tree.

## ACTIVITY TWIST

Vary this activity by writing down all the words relating to flowers, such as smell, petal, stem, or bug. This is a great spring or summer activity.

## POSTER POWER

189

*Any child who loves movies or videos will enjoy creating a colorful poster.*

**WHAT YOU'LL NEED:** newspapers or magazines, white paper, poster paper, markers or crayons, paints, paintbrush, other decorating materials, blunt scissors, clear tape or glue

Invite the child to choose a favorite movie or video. You may want to collect information about the star or movie in newspaper or magazine articles, if possible. Using the white paper, have the child write a summary or description of the movie or video. Provide the child with a list including stars, director, and others involved in the production. Include other information, such as reviews, that would encourage someone to buy a ticket to see the show.

Once the information has been gathered, help the child design the poster. Use paints, crayons, magazine pictures, or other materials to make the poster colorful and appealing. Display the finished poster in a prominent location. This activity can be modified to promote a book or favorite author.

## CLIFF-HANGER STORIES

190

*Promote story writing with this favorite form of story—the old-fashioned cliff-hanger.*

**WHAT YOU'LL NEED:** piece of paper, pencil, hanger, clothespins

Explain to the child what a cliff-hanger story is. If possible, rent some old movies that have cliff-hanger episodes or share a story that leaves the reader wanting more at the end of each chapter. Help the child write a cliff-hanger story, with cliff-hangers at the end of each chapter. Write the cliff-hanger on a piece of paper and clip to a hanger.

# ALPHABET OF YOU

191

*In this writing activity the child learns how to
use adjectives in an alphabet poem.*

**WHAT YOU'LL NEED:** paper, pencil, dictionary (optional)

Have the child begin by listing the letters of the alphabet. Talk about what an *adjective* is: a word that describes. Brainstorm a variety of positive adjectives that fit the child: *smart, curly-haired, inventive,* and so on. Have the child try to write one word for each letter of the alphabet. You may have to be inventive for *x: eXcellent* or *eXciting.* This is a great time to practice using a children's dictionary to look for appropriate words. Repeat this process another time using a different topic.

192

# REFRIGERATOR WRITING

*The refrigerator is not just for keeping things cool.
Use it to encourage writing, too.*

**WHAT YOU'LL NEED:** magnetic letters or word sets,
notebook, pencil

Fill the front of the refrigerator with the magnetic letters or words. Create some simple words on the refrigerator for the child to read and then copy them in a notebook. Then encourage the child to create words. Have the child copy these words in the same notebook. Invite the child to form sentences with words created. Use this as a time to reinforce spelling skills as well.

# WORD WHEEL

**193**

*Get rolling with word play in this activity, and explore words that move.*

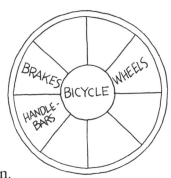

**WHAT YOU'LL NEED:** paper, pencil

Draw a picture of a wheel, using the example on the right as your guide. Be sure to include spokes and a round area in the center. Invite the child to choose something that moves, such as a bicycle, in-line skates, or wheelbarrow. Then have the child write the chosen word in the center of the wheel. Talk about all the words you can think of relating to that word. For example, a bicycle may include handlebars, brakes, seat, gears, and so on. Have the child write the related words between the spokes as shown.

**194**

# WORD COLLAGE

*Words take on a personality all their own when they are artistically arranged in a collage. Get creative!*

**WHAT YOU'LL NEED:** old magazines, blunt scissors, glue or clear tape, paper

Work with a variety of topics that contain words found in magazines. Good examples include food, fashion, sports, and music. Choose a topic. Then find all the related words in magazine headlines or in advertisements. Look for words in a variety of fonts, colors, and artistic treatments. Have the child cut out the words. Then invite the child to place the words on the paper and create new sentences, phrases, or interesting arrangements. Add appropriate punctuation to enhance the collage. Glue or tape all the pieces in place. If there is room, the child can add related pictures.

## 195 CREATING A TIME CAPSULE
▼▼▼▼▼▼▼▼▼▼▼▼▼▼▼▼▼▼▼▼▼▼▼▼▼

*In this activity, the child will have the opportunity to create his or her own legacy.*

**WHAT YOU'LL NEED:** airtight container, 3×5-inch index cards, pencil

Discuss what a time capsule is and how people enjoy seeing what life was like in the past. Find a container that will be safe for at least ten years: an airtight plastic container or a small fireproof box. Talk about what is important in the child's life right now. Have the child collect various items representing these times. For each item, help the child write a description on a card, including information about its use. Place the items in the box. Put a label on it that says "To be opened on _____" giving a date that is ten years in the future. Then put the time capsule in a safe place to be opened ten years later!

## WRITING TO A TEE! 196
━ ▪ ━ ▪ ━ ▪ ━ ▪ ━ ▪ ━

*This T-shirt will always be a child's pleasant reminder of a special event.*

**WHAT YOU'LL NEED:** white T-shirt, cardboard, permanent markers, 3×5-inch index cards (optional)

Choose a theme with the child, such as color words, or a special event, such as a birthday. Think of a list of words together that relate to the theme or event: *cake, candles, gifts, cards, balloons, party, friends, ice cream,* and so on. Encourage the child to arrange the words on a T-shirt by writing the words on cards and laying them on the shirt. Then place a piece of cardboard between the layers of the shirt. Invite the child to write words or draw illustrations on one side of the shirt with markers. Let dry thoroughly. Turn over and repeat process. Let dry and wear.

# SPELLING SPECIALS

Spelling instruction is most effective when it is integrated, or linked, with reading, language, science, social studies, math, art, or any other meaningful curriculum in which the child is interested. The activities in this chapter provide a variety of opportunities for the child to learn and apply basic spelling principles. The child will enjoy word puzzles such as Letter Tiles and Web Words and be intrigued with projects such as Break the Code and Invisible Words—all of which provide useful strategies for practicing spelling.

## INVISIBLE WORDS

*Spies and detectives have used this clever writing trick for years—invisible ink! Here's the secret recipe!*

**WHAT YOU'LL NEED:** saucer, lemon, cotton-tip swab, white paper, iron

Squeeze some lemon juice into a saucer. Invite the child to dip a cotton-tip swab into the lemon juice and write a sentence, or message, on white paper. Have the child use new spelling words in the sentence. Then watch. As the juice dries, it becomes virtually invisible! Next have the child give you the invisible message to see if it can be read. TOP SECRET TIP FOR ADULTS ONLY: To make the words reappear, place the message facedown on top of a old towel or rag. Iron the back of the paper with a warm iron. Share encoded message with the child and see how many words are spelled correctly.

# 198 — JUMPIN' JIMMINY

*The child will practice spelling words frequently used in reading and writing while jumping from X to X.*

**WHAT YOU'LL NEED:** masking tape, list of spelling words from school

Place masking tape X's in a path around the room. Have the child stand behind the first X. Explain that the object of this game is to move from X to X until the child reaches the end of the path. Begin by reading sight words for the child to spell. Focus on sight words the child uses frequently. Some examples may include: *the, come,* and *said.* For a correctly spelled word, the child jumps ahead one X. The child does not move if the word has been spelled incorrectly. For especially difficult words, you may offer two jumps ahead if it is spelled correctly. So get ready, get set, spell, and jump!

# COOKIE CUTTER WORDS — 199

*Here's a tasty way for the child to practice spelling theme-related words.*

**WHAT YOU'LL NEED:** prepared sugar cookie dough, floured surface, butter knife, cookie sheet, edible sprinkles, waxed paper or paper plate, spatula

Set out prepared cookie dough while discussing theme-related words and their meanings. Carefully cut the dough into letters. Have the child spell these theme-related words by arranging the cookie-dough letters on a cookie sheet. Invite the child to decorate the cookies before you bake them. Once the cookies have cooled, remove them from the cookie sheet and place on waxed paper or a paper plate. Review the spelling of each word with the child before enjoying the tasty spelling treat.

# CROSSWORD PUZZLES

**200**

*Across, down, this way and that, crossword puzzles make spelling old hat.*

**WHAT YOU'LL NEED:** graph paper with large squares

Invite the child to create a crossword puzzle using spelling words you and the child have chosen. The words may be ones the child has had difficulty spelling in daily writing, a spelling list from school, or new words the child wants to learn to spell. Help the child make the words fit on the graph paper, going across or down. Then on a separate sheet of paper, assist the child in writing a clue for each word. When the puzzle is finished, pass on to another person to solve.

**201**

# CHEER 'EM UP!

*Try this combination of markers and glitter to create a colorful, cheerful greeting.*

**WHAT YOU'LL NEED:** 8×10-inch posterboard folded in half, markers, glitter, glue, felt-tip pens

Invite the child to create a cheerful greeting card. Begin by having the child write the greeting on the front of the card in large, decorative letters. Then have the child write a short note to the recipient on the inside of the folded card. Next set out glitter, glue, and colored markers and encourage the child to decorate the card with a little color and sparkle. When the card is dry, it is ready to be given to that special someone who needs some cheer!

# PICTURE DICTIONARY

*This dictionary provides the child with a powerful tool for alphabetizing, spelling, and learning new words.*

**WHAT YOU'LL NEED:** several 18×6-inch strips of construction paper, markers, clear tape

Invite the child to make a picture dictionary of all new spelling words. Choose words from a school spelling list or words the child wants to learn to spell. Help the child tape 18×6-inch strips of paper end to end. Fold the strip back and forth, accordion-style, creating about three sections to each 18-inch strip. Make sure there are 26 pages. Then have the child decorate the book cover.

Next the child should write one letter of the alphabet from *Aa* to *Zz* on each page. The child can then write the spelling words on the appropriate page. You may want to help the child alphabetize the words before they are written in the picture dictionary. Finally help the child write a definition for each entry and encourage him or her to include a colorful illustration, too.

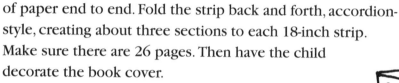

# STRETCH-A-WORD

**203**

*In this activity the child exercises the body and the mind for the sake of spelling.*

**WHAT YOU'LL NEED:** nine 11×17-inch pieces of colored construction paper, masking tape, markers

Tape colored paper on the floor to make a 3×3-square grid large enough for the child to stretch out on. Write the letters *a, b, d, f, n, m, p, s,* and *t,* in the squares on the grid. To play the game, say a three-letter word that has the short vowel *a* sound, such as *fan* or *nap.* Have the child spell the word by putting his or her foot on the first letter, the left hand on the second letter, and the right hand on the third letter.

## ACTIVITY TWIST

For a more challenging game, have the child spell four- or five-letter words, using both hands, both feet, and even his or her head!

# 204

# LETTER COLLAGE

*Encourage the young artist to create this letter collage while learning new spelling words.*

**WHAT YOU'LL NEED:** wallpaper, old magazines and newspapers, clear tape or glue, blunt scissors

Discuss words related to a current social studies or science theme. Then gather some old magazines and newspapers to look at. Have the child point to the individual letters needed to spell each theme-related word. Next cut out the letters the child has indicated. Help the child glue or tape the letters on sheets of patterned wallpaper to make creative theme collages.

# HIDDEN WORDS

# 205

*While learning to spell new words, the child will create a puzzle to challenge others.*

**WHAT YOU'LL NEED:** pencil, graph paper, list of spelling words

Provide a list of words that you would like the child to learn to spell. Then have the child write the words on graph paper, one letter in each square. The words can go across, down, or diagonally across the paper. Although some words may also share letters as they cross, make sure there are plenty of blank spaces.

When all of the words have been written on the graph paper, have the child write a letter in each blank space so that the entire puzzle is filled. Then have the child share the hidden word puzzle with a friend, asking him or her to find the words and circle them.

# PATTERN PLAY

## 206

*Improve the child's spelling abilities with this creative approach to analyzing spelling patterns.*

**WHAT YOU'LL NEED:** pipe cleaners

List words spelled with a similar pattern and invite the child to discover how they are alike. For example, the words *took* and *cook* have the spelling pattern *ook,* and the words *night* and *light* have the spelling pattern *ight.*

Next ask the child to form each letter in the pattern by bending and twisting pipe cleaners. Then make pipe cleaner letters to add to the pattern in order to spell new words with the same pattern. How many words can the child spell with the same spelling pattern?

## 207

# ABC ORDER

*A little word processing on the computer will add pizzazz to this ABC order activity!*

**WHAT YOU'LL NEED:** computer with word processor

ant
balloon
carrot

Invite the child to type words from a spelling list into the computer. Show the child how to highlight and move a word to a new location on the page. Then ask the child to put the words on the list in alphabetical order. The final product can be made to look creative by changing the type to a large, decorative font before printing.

# 208 LETTER TILES

*In this simple game, the child creates letter tiles to build spelling words!*

**WHAT YOU'LL NEED:** large index cards, markers

Help the child make three sets of letter tiles from index cards for the consonant clusters *gr, br,* and *fr.* Then make three sets of tiles for each individual letter of the alphabet, from *a* to *z*. Next invite the child to build words with the letter tiles. Encourage the child to build two words at a time, making sure that the words have at least one letter in common as shown. Then challenge the child to build three words at a time. Continue building words until all of the consonant clusters are used up.

## ACTIVITY TWIST

Once all the consonant clusters have been used up, help the child write sentences with the words made from the letter tiles.

# INVENTED WORDS

*The child will Zam! Pow! and Whamee! into spelling with this awesome cartoon lovers' activity.*

**WHAT YOU'LL NEED:** comic strips, paper, crayons, pencils, blunt scissors, construction paper

Review comic strips together, reading and enjoying the action. Look for words made up by the writer that express actions or feelings. Have the child cut out the action words and study them to discover the interesting ways in which they are spelled.

Next have the child make up his or her own comic words. Invite the child to make a cartoon with the invented words by writing the words in large, colorful letters on construction paper, such as the examples shown.

# ACTIVITY TWIST

Invite the child to create his or her own comic strip by drawing favorite or made-up characters to accompany the comic cartoons.

# BREAKFAST SPELLING

210

*Turn breakfast into a silly spelling event in which new words are sipped, slurped, or crunched.*

**WHAT YOU'LL NEED:** cereal with ABC pieces, milk, spoon, dish

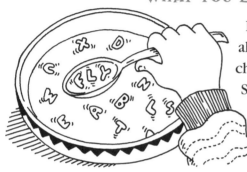

Pour fresh milk into two bowls that have been filled with alphabet cereal, one for the child and one for you. Invite the child to practice spelling words while eating the cereal. Scooping up the letters, arranging them on the spoon in the correct order, and reading the new word is a sure way to strengthen spelling skills while making breakfast a hilarious and educational event.

211

# BUILDING BLOCKS

*Wooden blocks become a motivating tool for the child to practice ing words.*

**WHAT YOU'LL NEED:** letter blocks

Set out blocks with letters on them. Have the child line up the blocks to form the word part *ing.* The child may gather the *s* block (*sing*), the *k* block (*king*), and other blocks to form words. It may be necessary to remind the child that when a word ends in *e,* he or she should drop the *e* before adding *ing,* as in *skate* and *skating* or *smile* and *smiling.* Try other spelling patterns for continued practice.

# BACKWARD BEE

**212**

*Spelling words backward is just as fun as spelling words forward. Try it and see!*

Begin by providing a list of words for the child to spell. They may be words from a school spelling list or words the child wants to learn to spell. Then, just like in a regular spelling bee, give the child the words to spell. However, instead of spelling the word forward, have the child spell it backward. The child gets one point for each word spelled correctly.

**213**

# SPELLING VOLCANO

*Engage the child in this challenging activity of wits and vocabulary.*

**WHAT YOU'LL NEED:** paper, pencil

Begin by drawing boxes in the shape of a volcano, like the example shown here, but don't fill in the letters: two boxes at the top, followed by a row of three boxes, a row of four boxes, a row of five boxes, and so on to seven. Then write a two-letter word on the top row, perhaps *an*. Have the child add one new letter to the previous word to spell a new word. Write the new word on the second row of the volcano. Continue in this way, adding one new letter each time, going as far down the volcano as possible. Can the child make it to the bottom?

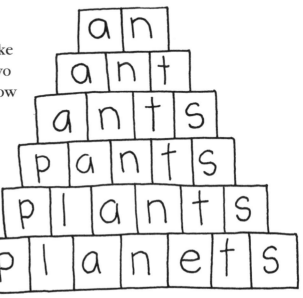

# BREAK THE CODE

*The child becomes a spelling sleuth while trying to break secret codes.*

**WHAT YOU'LL NEED:** felt-tip pens, blunt scissors, pencil, paper

Help the child make a code breaker. Begin by drawing a wheel pattern with felt-tip pens like the one shown here. Cut out the wheel. Write the letters of the alphabet in sequential order in the spaces on the outer edge of the largest wheel and their corresponding numbers, 1–26, on the inner wheel as shown.

Next write a secret message on a separate piece of paper in code; that is, substitute the corresponding number for each letter. Then the child can take on the role of a young sleuth and decode a secret message by using the code breaker. For example, using the encoder shown, the following message says:

13-5-5-20  13-5  1-20  20-8-5
6-15-18-20!

M-E-E-T  M-E  A-T  T-H-E  F-O-R-T!

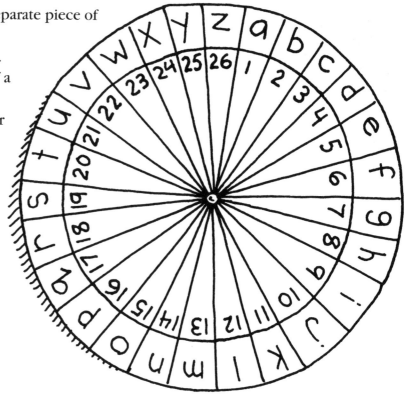

# APPLE TREE

**215**

*There is more to an apple tree when the child plays this version of the game of hangman.*

**WHAT YOU'LL NEED:** masking tape, paper, pencil

Before play begins, make a ladder with masking tape on a tile floor or smooth surface. Make five rungs on the ladder. Then draw an apple tree on paper. Next think of a specific spelling word, perhaps one from the child's weekly spelling list or a word the child may want to learn to spell. Then draw a row of apples on the tree.

Next have the child stand on the bottom rung of the ladder and try to guess one letter that is part of the word. Every correct letter gets written in the appropriate apple. For every incorrect guess, the child must step up one rung on the ladder. The game ends when the child guesses the spelling of the word correctly, or if he or she "steps off the top of the ladder." Ready to play again? Just erase the letters on the tree and start the game over.

**216**

# WORD SQUARE

*Here's a head scratcher that will keep the child thinking long after it is put down.*

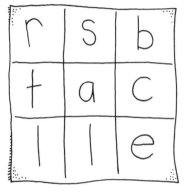

**WHAT YOU'LL NEED:** paper, pencil

Copy a word square like the one shown here on a piece of paper. Begin by having the child choose any letter in the puzzle and start building a word. Explain that each letter in the word being built must touch another letter in the square. To accomplish this the child can move up, down, across, or diagonally around the square. Demonstrate by spelling the word *ball*. Encourage the child to spell as many words as possible using the letters in the square.

# PASTA PIZZAZZ

**217**

*This entertaining spelling project allows the child to analyze spelling patterns while creating wearable art.*

**WHAT YOU'LL NEED:** rigatoni noodles (without ridges), strands of yarn, felt-tip pens

Ask the child to write the following words on separate noodles: *hen, pen, Ben.* String the noodles on a piece of yarn. Do the same for this next batch of words: *cake, wake, take.* Next set out a dish of noodles. Ask the child to look at the words on each strand, identify the spelling pattern (in this case *en* and *ake*), and make new word noodles to add to each. Help the child tie the finished strands to create wearable spelling art.

# ACTIVITY TWIST

For a challenging variation, invite the child to construct a sentence using as many words from the wearable art as possible. Expect some silly sentences.

# 218 GO FLY A KITE

*The child will enjoy practicing the* ite *spelling pattern while flying a kite.*

**WHAT YOU'LL NEED:** paper kite, 8½×11 pieces of paper, stapler, markers

Set out a paper kite. You may wish to make the kite from paper and wooden crossbars, or use a purchased model. Talk about kites with the child and explain what makes them fly. Discuss the importance of the tail.

Then have the child write the word *kite* on the body of the kite. Point out the letters *ite* in the word and explain that many other words are spelled with this pattern. Next have the child write other words that end with *ite* on pieces of paper, one word for each piece. Some *ite* words include: *bite, site, excite, invite, quite, recite, white,* and *polite.* Staple the paper pieces to the tail to make a high-flying kite. Then if it's a windy day, go outside and fly the kite together.

# POPCORN POETRY

**219**

*Popcorn Poetry is a contagiously funny way to review spelling patterns while writing poetry.*

**WHAT YOU'LL NEED:** index cards, markers, construction paper

Invite the child to help you make word cards for words that are spelled with the spelling pattern *ot*, such as *not, hot, got, pot,* and *dot.* Then copy the poem shown here on construction paper, leaving the spaces blank. Place the word cards randomly next to each line in the poem. Have the child read the *ot* words in the order they are listed.

Using the cards, invite the child to select the words so the poem makes sense, and place the word cards next to the appropriate sentences. Let the child have the honor of reading the finished poem aloud.

Pop! Pop! Pop! Pop the corn into the ____. [hot]

Pop! Pop! Pop! Take and shake it 'till it's ____. [got]

Pop! Pop! Pop! Lift the lid. What have we ____? [pot]

Pop! Pop! Pop! POPCORN! That's what !

# FLIP-FLOP WORDS

**220**

*The child will flip over this spelling puzzler!*

Did you know that some words, when spelled backward, spell another word? Try it and see. Begin by having the child spell *top.* Then invite the child to write the word again with the last letter first and the first letter last. What word did you spell? (*pot*) Try it again with *bus* (*sub*), and *pan* (*nap*). Continue by searching for new flip-flop words. Use a children's dictionary, if necessary.

# WEB WORDS

**221**

*This chip-flipping activity provides lots of practice spelling words with the short e sound.*

**WHAT YOU'LL NEED:** flat plastic chips, poster board, markers

Before beginning, help the child draw a large web on a piece of poster board like the one shown here. In each section of the web have the child draw a picture of an object spelled with a short *e*, as in *web*. To play the game, set two chips on a hard surface, such as a table or tile floor, next to the game board. Instruct the child to bounce the chip off the surface to make it jump or flip into the air. Watch as the chip lands on the web. The child may want to take a few practice flips. Then have the child say the name of the picture that the chip has landed on and spell it. Continue until all pictures are spelled.

# VERY PUNNY

**222**

*In the mood for a chuckle? Then jump right into this punny activity that focuses on homophones.*

**WHAT YOU'LL NEED:** paper, pencil or markers

Explain to the child that homophones are words that sound the same but are spelled differently, such as *to, two,* and *too.* Begin by making a list with the child of familiar homophones, such as *bear* and *bare.* Then invite the child to write and illustrate some puns. For example, the child may write "The boy has bear feet." Explain the difference between "bear feet" and "bare feet." Discuss which sentence is funnier and why. Invite the child to share his or her work with others.

# I SPY

▼▼▼▼▼▼▼▼▼▼▼▼▼▼▼▼▼▼▼▼▼▼▼▼▼▼▼▼▼▼▼▼

**223**

*I Spy something red, yellow, blue, green, and purple in the sky. The name has long a sound. What is it?*

This game is played using long *a* words, such as *cake, page,* and *rainbow.* Look around the room until you find an object with a long *a* sound in its name. Give one or more clues to help the child identify the object. Then have the child spell the name of the object. Once the child has correctly spelled the name of the object, encourage him or her to use the name of the object in a sentence.

## ACTIVITY TWIST

For a challenging variation, identify objects using other vowel sounds such as short *a*, short *e*, long *e*, and so on. Use as many vowel sounds as possible.

# CONTRACTION MATCH

## 224

*Practice recognizing contractions with this simple matching activity.*

**WHAT YOU'LL NEED:** 3×5-inch index cards, markers

Begin by making ten sets of contraction cards. Each set should consist of the contraction on one card and the words that make the contraction on the other. Use these example sets to get you started: *they'll* and *they will*; *can't* and *cannot*; *don't* and *do not*; *I'll* and *I will*. Next mix up the cards. Then invite the child to match a contraction with its correct counterpart words. When a match is found, have the child say what's on each card. After all the cards have been matched, invite the child to copy the contractions and the counterpart word cards into a personal dictionary.

## 225

# CROSSWORD BLOCKS

*These simple crossword puzzles require only the addition of one new letter to complete them.*

**WHAT YOU'LL NEED:** wooden letter blocks

Set out wooden letter blocks of consonants to form crossword puzzles like the one shown here. Ask the child to place one block in the center of the puzzle to complete the spelling of two different words, one going across and one going down (such as using the letter *e* to spell *bed* and *hen*). Encourage the child to create his or her own three-letter crossword puzzles. This activity can also be done with paper and pencil.

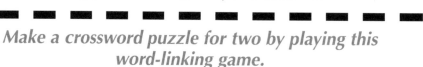

# CROSSED WORDS

**226**

*Make a crossword puzzle for two by playing this word-linking game.*

**WHAT YOU'LL NEED:** paper or graph paper, pencil, ruler

Begin by marking off a square that contains 15 boxes down and 15 boxes across, like the one shown here. Graph paper works best, but if you don't have any, use a ruler to draw the lines on a piece of blank paper. Outline the box in the center of the puzzle so it stands out.

Next choose a theme for the puzzle together, such as food, animals, and so on. Begin by thinking of one word that fits in the chosen category, and write the word on the page, one letter per box. The first word must have at least one letter that goes through the middle box. Then have the child think of a word within the category—the tricky part is that every word must share a letter with a word that's already on the page. Continue taking turns until neither you nor the child can think of any more words that will fit on the graph. See how close you both come to filling the puzzle.

ANIMALS

# MORSE CODE

227

*Once the child knows this spelling code, dots and dashes blossom into words!*

Explain to the child that in 1838, Samuel Morse created a special code that was named after him. In his code, a dot is a short tap and a dash is a long tap (with more time in between taps, that is). People used this code to send messages before telephones or radios. Morse designed his code so that the most often used letters in the alphabet have the shortest signals.

Begin by asking the child to choose a vocabulary word from a school spelling list or one the child wants to learn to spell. Then invite the child to tap out the correct spelling of the word on his or her knee. Have the child use a short tap for dots and a longer tap for dashes.

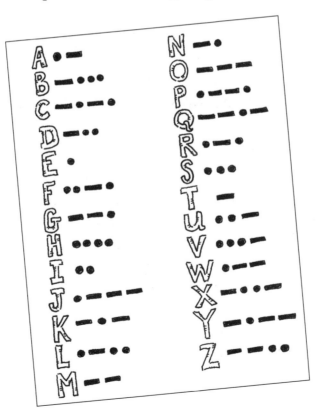

# PALINDROME PALS

**228**

*The child will want to back up and start again with this wacky activity that puts spelling in forward motion.*

Explain to the child that a palindrome is a word that is spelled the same forward or backward. Some examples are *mom* and *toot.* Invite the child to see how many palindromes he or she can come up with. Use the following clues to help the child get started: another name for father (*dad*); sound made by a baby chick (*peep*); sound made by a bursting balloon (*pop*); body part for seeing (*eye*); time in the middle of the day (*noon*).

**229**

# MAGIC WORDS

*Put a magic spell on some familiar words and turn them into new words. Just say "Abracadabra!"*

Pose the following question to the child: How do you turn a cap into a cape? The answer: With magic! A magic *e,* that is. Show the child how adding an *e* to some words will "magically" turn them into other words.

Next invite the child to put a magic spell on words such as *tub* and *cub,* turning them into the new words *tube* and *cube.* Ask the child to think of other words that could fall under the same spell. You may want to suggest the following words to get the child started: *tap, her, cut, kit, rip, rob,* and *can.*

# **230** **BACKWARD ALPHABET**

*If you think walking backward is difficult, try talking backward.*

**WHAT YOU'LL NEED:** watch with a second hand or a stopwatch, paper, pencil

Invite the child to say the alphabet from *A* to *Z*. Use a watch with a second hand or a stopwatch to time the child. Then have the child say the alphabet again, but this time in reverse, *Z* to *A*. Time this, also. Continue this several times in a row to see how fast the child can say the alphabet, forward and backward.

# **BONDED** **231**

*The object of this activity is to bond together
a word, forward and backward.*

**WHAT YOU'LL NEED:** paper, pencil

Begin by choosing a vocabulary word from the child's school spelling list or one the child wants to learn to spell. Make three vertical columns on a piece of paper. Write the chosen word down the left column, one letter atop the other. Next write the same word backward, last letter first, down the right column. Then take turns trying to "bond" the columns of letters together by adding whatever letters you or the child can think of in the middle column to spell words across. See if you can fill the middle column. The following example is for the word *horse.*

# MAGNETIC PERSONALITY

*The child will stick with this activity like a magnet to metal!*

**WHAT YOU'LL NEED:** magnetic letters, magnetic surface

Display magnetic letters on a magnetic surface, such as a refrigerator door, the front of the washing machine, file cabinet, a cookie sheet, or another safe metal object. Invite the child to rearrange the scrambled letters to make words from a spelling list that you have created or one the child has brought home from school. Help the child use the words in sentences.

## ACTIVITY TWIST

If you do not have magnetic letters, you can use game letter tiles, ABC cereal, or homemade letter flash cards.

# GRAMMAR GRABBERS

Taking an interactive approach to developing grammar, this chapter is jam-packed with creative, fun, hands-on projects that integrate spelling, usage, and vocabulary. The child will learn about nouns, verbs, pronouns, adjectives, and all the other essential grammar elements by getting involved in activities such as baking cookies in Bakery Nouns, making scrapbooks in Past Tense Sense, and much, much more. Sound like fun? It is! So get ready for a grammar extravaganza.

## 233 TEN QUESTIONS

*While enjoying this game of questions and answers, the child will develop sentence sense.*

Is it a toy?
Does it have wheels?
Can it be turned on and off?

**WHAT YOU'LL NEED:** small objects, bag or box, notebook paper, pencil

Place an object, such as a hairbrush, inside a bag or box. Invite the child to ask questions about the object in the bag in an effort to discover its identity. Write the questions on a piece of notebook paper, pointing out the capital letter at the beginning of each sentence and the question mark at the end, before answering them. A maximum of ten questions can be asked before the object is revealed; however, at any time during the question and answer exchange, the child can try to guess the object. If the child correctly identifies the object, a new object is placed in the bag and play is continued.

# PICTURE-GO-ROUND

**234**

*This picturesque activity forms the basis of grammar—*
*speaking and writing in complete sentences.*

**WHAT YOU'LL NEED:** old magazine, newspaper, or photo album; blunt scissors

Prepare for this activity by cutting out an interesting picture from an old magazine or newspaper or by removing one from a photo album. Invite the child to describe what is in the picture. Encourage the use of complete sentences. If necessary, assist the child in constructing complete sentences based on the words used to describe the picture. Explain that a sentence is a group of words that tell a complete thought. It must tell about someone or something (the subject) and what that person or thing is or does (the predicate). Repeat the activity using a different picture.

**235**

# BAKERY NOUNS

*Munching a bunch of sugar cookies is a yummy way for*
*the child to learn about nouns! See for yourself.*

**WHAT YOU'LL NEED:** prepared cookie dough, paper, sugar cookie recipe, cookie cutters, cookie sheet, pencil

If possible, visit a bakery to look at the shaped sugar cookies. Point out that bakers bake cookies in many shapes, such as stars, circles, hearts, squares, diamonds, and many others. Explain that the names of the cookie shapes are called *nouns.* Follow up by inviting the child to shape some cookies by hand with prepared cookie dough. Then have the child write the noun that names the cookie shape on a piece of paper. Next bake the cookies for the child, following the recipe's directions. Once the cookies have cooled, enjoy a tasty snack.

## 236 LOST AND FOUND

*Where, oh where, has my favorite
storybook character gone?*

**WHAT YOU'LL NEED:** favorite storybooks, construction paper,
crayons or markers

Place a few favorite storybooks in a quiet reading area and
provide ample time for the child to browse through the books
before you begin.

Begin by inviting the child to make a lost and found poster for a
storybook character. Encourage the child to describe the lost
character. Explain that the reader will want to know who is lost,
what they look like, and anything else about the character that
would help identify them. Allow the child to return to the book
area, if needed, to look for pictures of the selected character or to double-check information.

As the child works on the poster, have him or her include information as to what should be done if
the lost character is found. Encourage creative thinking and spontaneity as the child creates the poster.

## NAMES, NAMES, NAMES 237

*Get out your markers, and write up a stack of labels
for items around the house.*

**WHAT YOU'LL NEED:** 3×5-inch index cards, stickers, or sentence strips; markers; dictionary

Set out index cards, stickers, or sentence strips and a box of markers. Invite the child to make
labels for objects (nouns) in the house, such as furniture, a computer, items on a desk, and so on.
Encourage the child to use a dictionary for the correct spelling of the noun before writing it. Then
have the child display the labels beside the objects.

## 238 FARMING PLURALS

*Plural nouns are everywhere at Old MacDonald's Farm!*

Sing the song "Old MacDonald Had a Farm" with the child. Encourage the child to use creative expression to enhance the song, perhaps by adding animal sounds, movements, and facial expressions. Then help the child make a list of the plural animal nouns from the song, such as *cows, sheep,* and *pigs.*

Review the list with the child. Then ask which plurals were formed by adding *s? es?* Which plural noun is the same as the singular form? For additional creative fun, invite the child to illustrate as many nouns from the song as possible.

## GOING ON A TRIP

### 239

*Pack your bags and get ready to go on a trip to learn about nouns.*

Think of a place to go on an imaginary trip. Then have the child pack his or her "bags." Begin by listing items to pack. For example, start with something that begins with the letter *A,* such as an *apple.* Then have the child repeat the first item and add something that begins with *B.*

Play continues until the end of the alphabet is reached. If the child is unable to find an object that starts with a particular letter, skip to the next letter. Remind the child that the name of each item packed for the trip is a *noun.* For an additional challenge, see how many of the nouns packed for your imaginary trip the child can remember.

# I SPY #2

**240**

*A keen eye and a good set of clues are valuable
tools for this game of seeing and saying.*

Begin by inviting the child to define an *adjective.* Explain to the child that adjectives describe nouns by telling how many or what kind. Some examples of adjectives are: A *tiny* kitten, a *blue* ball, a *cold* day.

Have the child think of an object in the room. It must be an object that is clearly visible. Ask the child to help you guess the object by offering clues that describe it. Point out that the clues should include adjectives that describe color, size, shape, or some other characteristic about the object (noun).

**241**

# ADVERB CUE CARDS

*While retelling this story, the child will add flavor with
cue cards and sounds while learning about adverbs.*

**WHAT YOU'LL NEED:** construction paper, markers

Retell the story "The Three Billy Goats Gruff," emphasizing the words and phrases that tell where: on the hillside, over the bridge, under the bridge, across the planks, into the water, and others. Next have the child make cue cards that say *on, under, across,* and *over* and decide on appropriate sound effects for each.

Retell the story again. This time have the child hold up the cue cards at the appropriate time and add the designated sound effect. Explain to the child that words that tell when or where are called *adverbs.* Invite the child to make a list of adverbs they know.

# 242 TACO SURPRISE

▼▼▼▼▼▼▼▼▼▼▼▼▼▼▼▼▼▼▼▼▼▼▼▼▼

*Learning about nouns was never as much fun as it is in this taco surprise!*

**WHAT YOU'LL NEED:** taco ingredients (sour cream, lettuce, tomato, green pepper, cooked beef or chicken, olives, shredded cheese, taco sauce, taco shells), cooking utensils (spoon, knife, cookie sheet), plates, napkins

Help the child learn about *nouns* as you make tacos together. Begin by listing the materials you will need. Then have the child divide the materials into three noun groups: *ingredients, cooking utensils,* and *serving utensils.* Using the lists as guides, carefully gather the necessary materials and set them out on a table or other large work area. Take care to prepare the ingredients before you begin. To make the tacos, follow this simple recipe, adapting it to personal taste.

**Recipe:**

Fully cook beef or chicken, drain, and set aside.

Heat taco shells in warm oven for 3–5 minutes.

Spoon meat into bottom of heated taco shell.

Top with shredded lettuce, chopped tomatoes, chopped green peppers, sliced olives, shredded cheese, taco sauce, salsa, and sour cream.

Serve and eat!

| INGREDIENTS | COOKING UTENSILS | SERVING MATERIALS |
|---|---|---|
| sour cream | spoon | plates |
| lettuce | knife | napkins |
| tomato | cookie sheet | |
| green pepper | oven | |
| beef | pot holders | |
| chicken | | |
| olives | | |
| cheese | | |
| taco sauce | | |
| taco shells | | |

# 243 PROPER NOUN DRILL

*This simple activity based on proper nouns will teach the child how to react in an emergency situation.*

**WHAT YOU'LL NEED:** play telephone (or real telephone that is not connected), paper, pencil, index cards

Have the child write pertinent information on an index card so he or she knows how to answer the operator if a 911 emergency call has to be made. The information should include the child's name, address, and phone number. Explain that *proper nouns* are names of people, places, or things and begin with a capital letter. Have the child put the emergency information by the phone.

911 Information

Name-Jennifer Frank

Address-100 Your Street

Apartment 10A

Orlando, Florida

Phone- 555-4888

Using play telephones or a real phone that is not connected, have the child role-play calls to 911. You should play the role of the emergency operator, asking the child the nature of the emergency, his or her name, and address. The child may refer to the emergency card by the phone as needed.

**NOTE:**
Remind the child that he or she should only dial 911 on a real phone in the case of a real emergency.

# 244 GET IN THE ACTION

*A beloved Mother Goose rhyme becomes a foundation for teaching verbs.*

Sing a few verses of "Here We Go 'Round the Mulberry Bush" with the child. Invite the child to pantomime the actions. Explain that a word describing action is called a *verb*. Then have the child create his or her own verse, following the examples below. Ask the child what verb(s) he or she pantomimed in the verse.

Here we go 'round the mulberry bush,

the mulberry bush, the mulberry bush.

Here we go 'round the mulberry bush,

So early in the morning.

Verse 2. This is the way we wash our hands.

Verse 3. This is the way we wash our clothes.

Verse 4. This is the way we go to school.

Verse 5. (Make up a verse.)

# PAST TENSE SENSE 245

*The child will identify and use past tense verbs while creating a decorative scrapbook page!*

I skied down Sugar Mountain.

**WHAT YOU'LL NEED:** scrapbook page (or heavy paper), photo (or drawing) of the child, clear tape or glue

Help the child make a scrapbook page. Begin by having the child tape the picture or drawing on the page. Encourage the child to decorate the page using one or more of the following suggestions: paint a border, glue or tape a paper frame around the picture, use fancy letters to write a caption, add ticket stubs or other souvenirs associated with the picture. Invite the child to write a sentence at the bottom of the scrapbook page to show what happened. Remind them to write in the past tense.

# CHART SMART

*Need a spark for teaching adjectives? Try this simple sentence-building activity.*

Look at the chart shown here. Invite the child to build sentences using one word from each row. Have the child choose a word from the first line and write it on a piece of paper. Then have the child choose a word from the second line to follow the first word. Continue in this manner for the third and fourth lines. Next have the child read the completed sentence aloud. Point out the words that describe size and shape. Explain to the child that descriptive words are called *adjectives.* Repeat the activity several times.

One, The, Some
bus, whale, volcano, flower, dinosaur, snowflake
is, are
big, little, giant, tiny, yellow, gray, red

247

# 20 SECONDS

*The spotlight is on verb tenses in this memory-teasing activity.*

There were six beads on a necklace.

**WHAT YOU'LL NEED:** several small items (jewelry, pens, beads, spools of thread, etc.), tray

Play a memory game for the child to practice correct usage of the verbs *was* and *were*. Place one to three items on a tray in plain view of the child. Remove the tray from view after 20 seconds and have the child describe what the objects looked like. Encourage him or her to use the words *was* and *were* in the sentence.

# DIAMOND POEM

*While composing this poem about a favorite pet, the child will use words that are real gems!*

**WHAT YOU'LL NEED:** posterboard, markers

Invite the child to write a poem about a favorite pet in the shape of a diamond as shown. Help the child write the poem by following these line-by-line instructions.

Line 1—Kind of pet

Line 2—Two adjectives that describe the pet's shape or size

Line 3—Three verbs that end with *ing* and tell what the pet does

Line 4—Four nouns that name what the pet likes

Line 5—Three verbs that end with *ing* and tell what the pet does, but are different than Line 3.

Line 6—Two adjectives that describe the pet's personality

Line 7—Name of pet

Invite the child to share the poem with you. Then look at the poem again with the child, pointing out the *nouns.* Look again for *verbs,* and then for *adjectives.* You should find an abundance of each.

Hamster
tiny, chubby,
hiding, running, chewing,
carrots, lettuce, apples, oats,
gnawing, nibbling, squeaking,
sweet, shy
Furball

# 249 MUSEUM DISPLAY

*Here's an activity that lets the child create a mini museum while learning about adjectives.*

**WHAT YOU'LL NEED:** 3 shelves or tables, heavy paper

Discuss the art, science, or history museums you or the child have visited in the past and what was seen at each. Then help the child create a museum display by labeling exhibit areas as *People, Places,* and *Things.* You may want to use empty shelves in a bookcase as your display area. Other good display areas include windowsills, cardboard boxes, and tabletops.

Next have the child arrange collections of appropriate objects, such as stuffed animals and pictures, for each shelf in the display. It might be fun to set museum tour hours and then invite family members or friends to visit the museum. The child may want to act as a museum curator during the visits. Tell the child that a tour guide is someone who explains the exhibits to the visitors and answers their questions.

## ACTIVITY TWIST

To get a better understanding of how a museum tour guide does his or her job, take the child on a trip to a real museum and view a special exhibit.

# 250 QUESTIONS AND ANSWERS

*While tossing cotton balls from dish to dish, the child
will practice complete sentences. Try it and see!*

**WHAT YOU'LL NEED:** 2 large bowls, cotton balls, spoon, blindfold

Begin by blindfolding the child and handing him or her a spoon. Tell the child to scoop cotton balls out of one bowl and put them in the other in one minute. Sounds easy, doesn't it? But it's not. After the time limit expires, have the child count the cotton balls in the second bowl and the ones that missed. Next have the child answer these questions: Did you like this game? Why or why not? Did you think this game was hard? Why or why not? Encourage the child to use complete sentences.

# FUZZY, BRISTLY WORDS 251

*The child may feel itchy or bumpy all in the
name of learning adjectives.*

**WHAT YOU'LL NEED:** common household materials with different textures (rough sandpaper, silky satin, soft cotton, scratchy scrub pad, bristly brush, two-sided tape, smooth rock, and so on), large bag or box, blindfold

Before you begin, explain that *adjectives* are words that describe *nouns.* Then draw a word web (see page 141) and write the sentence "It feels _____" in the center. Blindfold the child and instruct him or her to place one hand inside a bag filled with textured objects. Ask the child to describe how the objects feel. Write the words the child uses on the web. Can the child guess what objects are in the bag?

## 252 WIND WAVERS

▼▼▼▼▼▼▼▼▼▼▼▼▼▼▼▼▼▼▼▼▼▼▼▼▼▼▼

*The child will be blown away by the wind in this
interactive grammar activity.*

**WHAT YOU'LL NEED:** crepe paper streamers or silk scarves

Have the child think of *adjectives* that describe the wind. List the words on a piece of paper to create a word list. Label the list "Adjectives for the Wind." Then invite the child to hold silk scarves and move about as though being blown gently by the wind.

Invite the child to describe how the wind feels. Perhaps words such as *breezy, wild, light, lofty,* or *soft* describe the wind. Then have the child add the new adjectives to the word list.

### ACTIVITY TWIST

After the child describes the wind, invite him or her to describe other elements in nature, such as rain and snow. Make corresponding lists for those adjectives, too.

# WALDORF SALAD

*The child will enjoy learning about verbs while you chop, slice, and mix a Waldorf Salad.*

**WHAT YOU'LL NEED:** apple, celery, nuts, mayonnaise or salad dressing, lettuce, nutcracker, knife, spoon, bowl, paper, pencil

Set out an apple, a stalk of celery, and some nuts. Ask the child to use simple words to tell what you might do to each of the foods before you eat them. Make a list of the action verbs suggested by the child, and identify them as such. Then carefully prepare the ingredients to make the following recipe for a Waldorf salad.

wash
peel
cut
chop

**Mix together:**

—1 chopped apple

—1 stalk sliced celery

—½ cup chopped nuts

—½ cup lite mayonnaise or salad dressing

Serve on a bed of lettuce.

# PUPPET EXTRAVAGANZA

*Raise the curtain on pronoun use in this puppet extravaganza.*

**WHAT YOU'LL NEED:** finger puppets (from page 210)

Both you and the child will enjoy using finger puppets to act out a favorite story, perhaps *The Three Little Pigs.* As you take on the roles of specific characters, remind the child to use pronouns such as *me, I, our,* and *us* when talking about themselves. Make sure the correct forms of the pronouns are used.

# UNDER THE LENS

*Get in touch with nature with this magnificent magnifying lens and look at the environment.*

**WHAT YOU'LL NEED:** magnifying lens

Have the child practice using the verbs *see* and *saw* correctly. Then go on a walking field trip. Walk around the block, through a park, into a forest or wooded area, on the shore, or in another natural area. Invite the child to look through a magnifying lens to help observe, or *see,* the surrounding environment. Encourage the child to use the words *see* and *saw* correctly while describing new discoveries. Then have the child record the discoveries, or what he or she *saw,* in a nature journal or notebook.

# JUST FOR THE TASTE OF IT!

**256**

*The child will eat adjectives with this tasty activity.*

**WHAT YOU'LL NEED:** lemon, salted peanuts, jelly beans, pretzels, and other foods

sour
lemon
salty
peanuts
sweet
jelly beans

Display common foods that include a wide variety of tastes, perhaps jelly beans, lemons, pretzels, marshmallows, peanuts, raisins, sour apples, or sweet banana peppers. Let the child sample the foods and describe how they taste. Record the words the child uses. Did he or she use words such as *sour, sweet, tangy, spicy, salty, delicious,* or *tasty*? Explain that these descriptive words are called *adjectives.* Invite the child to add more adjectives to the list. See how many he or she can think of.

## **257** WEATHER REPORT

*Amateur weather forecasters take over the weather reporting
for the day in this adjective-based activity.*

**WHAT YOU'LL NEED:** construction paper, markers, map (optional), pointer, table, old magazines

Allow the child to take on the role of weather forecaster for the day. As the child prepares to report the weather, have him or her make a list of *adjectives* describing different weather conditions, such as *sunny, rainy, windy, cloudy, snowy, hot, cold,* and so on. Provide materials to make props, such as pictures to represent the weather symbols, maps, and photographs. Encourage the young forecaster to use a pointer to use with the props to make the presentation more visual.

### ACTIVITY TWIST

Review verbs by having the child name activities he or she likes to do on sunny, snowy, rainy, or windy days.

# 258 YAK-A-SAK!

*Combining sentences from random sentence parts is a hilarious way to practice building sentences.*

**WHAT YOU'LL NEED:** 2 sacks, sentence strips

Begin by writing sentence parts on sentence strips. Make up five to six simple subjects, or naming parts. An example of a subject is: *red juicy tomatoes.* Write five to six simple predicates, or telling parts. An example of a predicate is: *are growing in the garden.* Place the two sentence parts in separate sacks. Next have the child pick one sentence part from each sack and combine them to make a sentence. Prepare yourself for some silly sentences.

## ACTIVITY TWIST

For additonal creative fun, invite the child to illustrate the silly sentences with pencils or crayons.

# 259 DIVING DEEP FOR NOUNS

*See and write about what's at the bottom of the sea while studying nouns.*

**WHAT YOU'LL NEED:** 5×40-inch white construction paper (or two 5×20 strips taped together end-to-end), crayons

Help the child fold the strip of white construction paper back and forth to create an eight-page accordion-fold book. Set the book aside. Sing the song "There's a Hole in the Bottom of the Sea" with the child. Then count how many nouns are in the bottom of this sea together. Name them: *hole, log, bump, frog, fly, wing, flea.* Invite the child to complete the accordion-fold book by humorously illustrating all of the nouns in the song. After the illustrations are finished, have the child unfold the pages of the book, one by one, to show each illustration as you both sing the song again.

# OPPOSITE DAY 260

*Say just the opposite of what you mean in this contagiously funny activity.*

Declare the day, "Opposite Day." Think of what you want to say, and then say the opposite. For example, if you want to say "Hello" to someone, you would instead greet them with "Goodbye." If you wanted to thank someone for turning off the light, you would say "You're welcome for turning on the dark."

# TRAVEL POSTER

*Visit faraway countries, interesting cities, or other travel destinations without leaving home. Here's how.*

**261**

**WHAT YOU'LL NEED:** posterboard, markers, scrap art materials, clear tape or glue, blunt scissors, old magazines

Help the child think of words that describe nouns. Explain that these descriptive words are called *adjectives*. Next invite the child to make a travel poster that encourages his or her friends to visit a new place. The travel destination may be a place the child has actually visited or a place he or she would like to travel to one day. The destination may be a country, state, city, or specific tourist attraction. To make the travel poster, help the child cut out pictures from old magazines of sights a traveler would want to see while visiting a chosen destination, or make inviting pictures from scrap art materials. Then tape or glue the pictures on the posterboard. Remember, the pictures should describe the location in a way that would motivate others to want to travel there. Once the pictures have been placed, have the child write phrases using colorful adjectives that describe the destination.

# MONTH AT A GLANCE

**262**

*The child will practice using and learning new nouns while creating this lively calendar.*

**WHAT YOU'LL NEED:** poster board, construction paper, felt-tip pens, ruler, old magazines, blunt scissors, clear tape or glue

Help the child make a calendar for one month by drawing a 7×5-inch grid on a piece of poster board. Have the child write the name of the month and the days of the week on the calendar. Remind the child that names of days are proper nouns and should begin with capital letters. Help the child number the days from 1 to 28, 29, 30, or 31. Make the calendar lively with cutouts and pictures to mark special days and events.

**263**

# MIME TIME

*In this activity, children will take on the role of mimes to act out verbs for an audience.*

**WHAT YOU'LL NEED:** white gloves, top hat, envelope or box, slips of paper, pencils

Have children write an action word (verb) on a slip of paper. Invite them to share the words they wrote and tell which word is a verb. Then have them place the slips of paper in an envelope or box.

Next invite one child to take on the role of a mime, slipping on white gloves and a hat. Explain that a mime is an actor who mimics or pantomimes people, animals, or events. The mime can use hand and facial gestures, body movements, and props, but cannot speak. Instruct the mime to pick a slip of paper from the box and act out the action. Invite children to guess the action. The first person who guesses the verb becomes the next mime.

## ACTION FIGURES

**264**

*Cartoon characters provide lots of opportunities to be exposed to common and proper nouns.*

**WHAT YOU'LL NEED:** large piece of construction paper, crayons or markers

Discuss the child's favorite action characters from TV and the movies. Invite the child to draw the characters on a large piece of construction paper. Then have the child write the name of each character above the corresponding drawing. Below the drawing, have the child write what kind of creature the character is. While looking at the picture, point out the differences between common nouns and proper nouns.

**265**

## CREATE-O-SAURUS

*Create your very own noun with this word-origin activity.*

**WHAT YOU'LL NEED:** drawing paper, crayons

Write the words *brontosaurus, tyrannosaurus,* and *stegosaurus* on paper. Then ask the child: What do all these words have in common? (They are all dinosaurs, nouns, and they all contain the word part *saurus*.) Explain that the word *saurus* means large lizard. Encourage creative thinking by having the child create and draw new dinosaurs and name them. Remind them to use the word part *saurus* in the dinosaur name.

# 266 HUMPTY DUMPTY'S FALL

•••••••••••••••••••••••••••••••••

*Experiment with* is *and* are *while answering questions about favorite nursery rhyme characters.*

Invite the child to act out traditional nursery rhymes, such as "Jack Be Nimble," "Three Blind Mice," "Jack and Jill," and "Humpty Dumpty." Pause from time to time to ask the child how the character or characters feel. Have the child answer the questions using the verbs *is* or *are*. After several responses, ask if the child sees a pattern for using *is* and *are*. Explain that singular subjects name one thing and plural subjects name more than one thing. The verb *is* is used with a singular subject: Humpty Dumpty *is* sad when he falls off the wall. The verb *are* is used with a plural subject: Jack and Jill *are* hurt when they tumble down the hill.

# 267 — HUNG OUT TO DRY

*Come join the three little kittens in their
search for sentence order.*

**WHAT YOU'LL NEED:** large index cards, clothesline, clothespins

Read or chant the familiar nursery rhyme "Three Little Kittens" with the child. The first verse of
the rhyme is shown below. Choose one or two sentences from the rhyme and write the words on
individual cards. Mix up the cards. Then have the child arrange and hang the cards on the clothesline
in sequential order to make complete sentences.

Three little kittens they lost their mittens,
And they began to cry,
"Oh, mother dear, we sadly fear
That we have lost our mittens."

"What! lost your mittens, you naughty kittens!
Then you shall have no pie."
Mee-ow, mee-ow, mee-ow.
No, you shall have no pie.

# BRIGHT IDEA

*The child will be caught hook, line, and sinker with this bright idea for reviewing nouns and verbs.*

**WHAT YOU'LL NEED:** large paper, crayons

Explain to the child that some words in our language can be both a noun and a verb. For example, write the word *fish*. The word can be a noun that names an animal that swims in the water. It can also be a verb that means to drop a line with a hook in the water so one is able to catch the scaly animal. Write the word *slide*. Ask the child what the word means when used as a noun. When is it used as a verb?

Set out paper and crayons. Invite the child to make a poster or banner by writing and drawing words that can be either a noun or a verb, such as *fish, slide,* and *paint.* Invite the child to think of other words to add to the poster.

# ACTIVITY TWIST

For a fun and challenging way to use words that are both a noun and a verb, help the child write a sentence that contains both forms.

# 269 HAPPY ABOUT VERBS

*Clap, tap, stomp, laugh, and sing until you're happy about verbs!*

Clap your hands and tap your feet as you join in the fun while singing the first verse of "If You're Happy and You Know It" with the child.

*If you're happy and you know it clap your hands. (clap, clap)*

*If you're happy and you know it clap your hands. (clap, clap)*

*If you're happy and you know it,*

*Then your face will surely show it!*

*If you're happy and you know it clap your hands. (clap, clap)*

Invite the child to write new verses for the song. Help the child think of new actions to replace clapping hands, such as stamping or tapping feet or moving the arms. Point out that the name for each action is a *verb*. Next sing the new verses the child has suggested, and sing until you're happy!

# LISTENING LAUNCHES

Listening involves the ability to hear and distinguish sounds in words, a skill necessary when translating written symbols into sounds and words, which is the foundation of reading. Through listening, the child will not only develop these abilities but will increase vocabulary skills and learn the building blocks of verbal communication. Included in this chapter are a wide variety of activities that offer the child an opportunity to develop some of the many aspects of good listening skills and to have fun engaging in challenging activities at the same time.

## 270 WHAT'S THE LETTER?

*This guessing game is a simple phonics activity that can be done anytime or anywhere. It's great for traveling.*

Begin by pointing to an object in the room or a picture in a magazine or book. Say the name of the object (person, animal, tree, flower, etc.). Ask the child to name the beginning letter. Continue to offer new items for letter guessing, or invite the child to choose an object and give you a turn at guessing.

To increase the difficulty of the game, offer a two- or three-word description of the object and ask the child to say the first letter of the object. The more unusual the items chosen for the game, the more interesting the game can be!

# 271 ONE WORD SWAPS

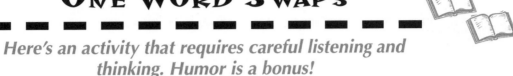

*Here's an activity that requires careful listening and thinking. Humor is a bonus!*

Begin by making up a sentence and writing it on a piece of paper. Make sure the sentence has an interesting subject, mentions a place, and contains an activity. (Example: I walked to the park and saw a tree.) Before slowly reciting the sentence to the child, ask him or her to listen carefully in order to repeat it. Explain that after you say the sentence, the child should change one of the words to a different word and then repeat the sentence in its slightly altered form. Any word in the sentence can be changed, as long as the sentence still makes sense. (Example: I walked to the park and saw a dog.) The more the meaning of the sentence changes, or the funnier it gets, the better.

After the child has changed a word and recited the sentence revision, write the revision underneath the original. Then take another turn yourself, and change a different word. (Example: I ran to the park and saw a dog). Continue taking turns, changing a different word each time. The game ends when every word in the original sentence has been changed.

## EXAMPLE:

I walked to the park and saw a tree.

I walked to the park and saw a dog.

I ran to the park and saw a dog.

I ran to the beach and saw a dog.

Mom ran to the beach and saw a dog.

Mom ran to the beach and heard a dog.

Mom ran along the beach and heard a dog.

Mom ran along the beach and heard two dogs.

Mom ran along a beach and heard two dogs.

Mom ran along a beach then heard two dogs.

# FISHING FOR RHYMES

272

*Practice indentifying rhymes when playing this modified version of Go Fish.*

**WHAT YOU'LL NEED:** 30 index cards, crayons or markers

Use index cards to create a deck of rhyming cards. The deck should be made up of 15 or more rhyme pairs, such as *cat/hat, bug/rug,* and *car/star*—one word for each card, 30 cards in all. When the deck is complete, pass out four cards to each player. Explain that the object of the game is to be the first person to get two pairs of rhyming cards.

Begin the game by asking the child for a card that rhymes with a card in your hand. For example, if you have a *hat* card, you would ask: "Do you have a rhyme for hat?" If the child has a card that rhymes, he or she must give up that card. If not, you may draw a new card from the deck. For every card picked from the deck, one must be discarded and placed at the bottom of the deck.

# ACTIVITY TWIST

Once the game is finished, encourage the child to create sentences that use one pair of rhymes in each sentence.

## 273 RHYME-A-STORY

*By listening for rhymes, the child will practice comprehension while creating a story.*

Make up a story together but tell it in rhymes. Begin by making up the first sentence. For example, you might say "The dog went for a walk." Then invite the child to make up a rhyming sentence, then another sentence for you to rhyme. Explain to the child that his or her second sentence does not have to rhyme with his or her first sentence. For example, the child would add "The dog began to talk. Then the dog began to run." Then you would continue with: "He wanted to get out of the sun. He found a tree to lay under." Continue until you and the child are satisfied with the ending.

## DO YOU REMEMBER? 274

*Sharing facts with the child is an interesting exercise to enhance listening and strengthen memory.*

Begin by telling ten things about yourself to the child. Your list may include such things as "I like dogs," "yesterday I ate spaghetti for dinner," or "the red shirt I am wearing is the one Grandma gave me." Then invite the child to tell ten personal facts as well.

After both of you have recited a list of ten personal facts, take turns trying to remember and repeat as many of the statements from the other person's list as possible.

# 275 POEM PYRAMIDS

▼▼▼▼▼▼▼▼▼▼▼▼▼▼▼▼▼▼▼▼▼▼▼▼▼▼▼▼

*Practice learning initial sounds of words with these simple sound poems.*

The structure for these sound poems is that each poem has only four lines. The first line has one word, the second line has two, the third line has three, and the fourth line has four. Each line includes the words of the line before it and adds one new word. The tricky part is that all words must begin with the same letter! See the example.

Begin by choosing a letter, or inviting the child to choose a letter, and create a poem pyramid together. After finishing the first poem, invite the child to create a new poem independently, using a different letter.

**EXAMPLE:**

Bee

Buzzy Bee

Big Buzzy Bee

Big Buzzy Bee Bumbling

# WHO'S TALKING? 276

▬ ▬ ▬ ▬ ▬ ▬ ▬ ▬ ▬ ▬ ▬ ▬ ▬

*In order to guess who's telling a story, the child will need to analyze information while listening.*

Retell a story or folktale that both you and the child are familiar with. This time, however, pretend that you are one of the characters in the story as you are telling it. Don't tell which character you are, but tell the story from that character's point of view! Then challenge the child to guess which character is telling the story.

# WHAT IS IT?

## 277

*Increase vocabulary and strengthen listening skills by playing this descriptive word game.*

Describe a familiar person, place, animal, or object using only single descriptive words—no sentences. List four or five descriptive words that relate to the item and then challenge the child to guess what it is. If you were thinking of a pet rabbit, for example, you may describe it as "furry, white, soft, small, and friendly." What is it?

# ACTIVITY TWIST

Once the child has guessed what the object is, encourage the child to create a sentence using the name of the object and as many of the descriptive words as possible.

# STORY CHORUS

● ● ● ● ● ● ● ● ● ● ● ● ● ● ● ● ● ● ● ● ● ● ● ● ● ●

**278**

*Creating sound effects to represent a story character is a wonderful way to engage the child in a favorite story.*

**WHAT YOU'LL NEED:** favorite book or story, sound-makers (key chain, whistle, jar of beans, musical instrument, etc.)

Begin by helping the child choose a story that has several major characters. Invite the child to choose a sound-maker for each one of the characters. The sound-makers may include musical instruments, a jar of beans, a whistle, or even foot-stomping. After each character's sound has been determined, read the story to the child. Each time the name of a particular character is mentioned, the child should make the appropriate sound.

**279**

# WHO AM I?

■ ▬ ■ ▬ ■ ▬ ■ ▬ ■ ▬ ■ ▬ ■

*In this guessing game, the child collects information and draws conclusions from verbal clues.*

Choose a character from a favorite story or fairy tale that both you and the child are familiar with. Then tell the child to pretend that you are one of the storybook characters. Invite the child to determine who you are by asking you *yes* or *no* questions for clues. Before the child begins asking questions, you may want to provide one or two clues to get started.

# 280 LISTENING WALK

*Describing everyday sounds engages the child's attention while enhancing language development.*

**WHAT YOU'LL NEED:** paper, pencil

Go on a listening walk with the child around the neighborhood, or even just around the house. Before you start, have the child write down all the sounds on a piece of paper that might be heard while walking. Then go on the walk.

Walk quietly together. Don't talk. Just listen carefully. Write down all the sounds you hear. When you return, check the list. How many items on the list did the child hear while walking? What did the child hear that was not on the list? Ask the child to describe each sound that was heard on the walk.

# ACTIVITY TWIST

For a creative challenge, invite the child to make up a story that includes some or all of the sounds on the list.

# DO AS I SAY!

**281**

*This direction-following activity is fun, challenging, and enhances listening skills.*

Following directions involves several different skills including listening, comprehending, remembering, and translating words into action. Begin by explaining that you are going to list several directions for the child to follow, and that each direction should be followed exactly in the order given. Start by giving only three or four directions at a time for the child to follow. For example, you may say "jump six times, turn all the way around, then touch your toes." After the child has shown that three or four directions can easily be followed, increase the difficulty by giving five directions in a series, and then six.

# SECRET WORD

282

*Listening for verbal clues helps determine the meaning of unknown words.*

Choose a word and keep it a secret. It must be a common word that is used often, such as *water* or a pet's name. Then agree on a sound for the secret word together—for example, tapping your foot or whistling. Then each time the word comes up in conversation, you will perform the signal. The game can take place during other activities such as preparing lunch, cleaning the house, or taking a walk. How long does it take the child to determine what the secret word is?

283

# WHAT WAS THAT SOUND?

*This simple game enhances the child's listening skills and can be played anytime.*

Have the child close his or her eyes and listen carefully. Then make a sound by using a common household item: shake a key chain, switch a light off and on, open and close a drawer, or rapidly flip through the pages of a book. After you have made the sound, ask the child to guess the name of the object making the sound.

# NONSENSE RHYMES

**284**

*The child will use knowledge of letter sounds when making up silly nonsense words and rhymes.*

Begin by offering a simple word, then invite the child to create a nonsense word that rhymes with it. For example, *jat* is a nonsense rhyme for the word *cat*, and *rish* is a nonsense rhyme for the word *fish*. Next suggest words with more than one syllable.

After the child has become comfortable making up nonsense rhyming words, make the activity more challenging by providing a sentence to be "nonsensically" transformed. Invite the child to turn as many words in a sentence into a nonsense word that rhymes with the word it will replace. For example, the sentence "A caterpillar crawled on a tree" could be "nonsensically" transformed into "A fraterpillar jawled on a cree."

**285**

# RECORD A STORY

*Create a personally taped version of a favorite story for independent listening!*

**WHAT YOU'LL NEED:** tape recorder

Choose a story that you or the child can retell and record. You may want to record an original story, one that you and the child make up, or even one that the child makes up. You can retell the story alone, recite it with the child, or invite the child to retell the story alone. You'll end up with endless listening pleasure. Remember, the most successful young readers are those who listen to stories often.

# STOP & GO STORIES

**286**

*Stop and go stories are a fun way for the child to focus on words during a narration.*

Invite the child to tell a story. The child can retell a favorite story or fairy tale, or make up a story. Before the child begins, explain that during the story you will be giving STOP and GO directions, and the child must stop telling the story the moment you utter the word STOP. The child may not continue the story until you say GO. As soon as you say GO, the child must begin the story right where he or she had stopped with the very next word that follows the last word said, even if that means beginning in midsentence. Challenge the child to tell the story from beginning to end without losing his or her place in spite of all the stop and go sounds.

**287**

# WHAT'S SILLY?

*Listening for what's silly in a story gives the child the experience of listening actively with purpose.*

Make up a story that includes three or four nonsensical things and tell it to the child. For example, you might say, "I slept late and didn't get out of bed until noon. I would have slept later but the hooting of the owls woke me up. As soon as I got out of bed, I took my shoes off and went into the bathroom to brush my face and wash my teeth. When I was finished, I put the soap back in the soap dish and put fresh toothpaste on my toothbrush. Then I went downstairs to make a bowl of cereal for my dinner."

After you finish telling the story, ask the child to name as many silly things in the story as possible. After that, the child may enjoy taking a turn telling a story with some silly things for you to catch.

# GUESS THAT WORD!

**288**

*This simple guessing game encourages the child to use limited information to guess a word in a category.*

Before beginning, choose a category together, such as food, places, or animals. Explain to the child that you are going to think of one item in that category and ask the child to do the same. For example, if the category is food you might choose apple pie and the child might choose pizza. Whatever the item is, do not reveal what you have chosen. The object of the game is to guess the other person's word before they guess yours. Each person takes a turn asking one question, listening to the response, and making one guess.

**289**

# TURNAROUND SOUNDS

▼▼▼▼▼▼▼▼▼▼▼▼▼▼▼▼▼▼▼▼▼▼▼▼▼▼

*Turning around sounds enhances the child's listening skills with a little help from phonics.*

Rearrange the letters of a word to make it into a different word. For example, the word *spoon* can be rearranged to *snoop, star* can be changed into *rats,* and *charm* can be changed into *march.* Think of a word that can be rearranged and tell the child the new word along with a clue to the original word. You may say, "If you turn around the letters and sounds, you can eat with a 'snoop.' What is the word?" Invite the child to rearrange the letters and sounds and try to figure out the correct word. You may want to write the new word on a piece of paper so the child can write different arrangements, too.

# ACT IT OUT

**290**

*This engaging activity inspires creative movements to accompany attentive listening.*

In this activity, the child can act out a favorite story by creating movements, gestures, or dramatizations. Encourage the child to listen carefully as you sing the words to a song. While you are singing, have the child create movements, gestures, or dramatizations for each verse. Make sure you take note of each gesture or movement. After the movements have been created, invite the child to sing as well as act out the song with the appropriate gestures and movements.

# 291 — SYLLABLE TALLY

*The child will enjoy rhythmic play while practicing breaking words into their sound parts.*

Teach the child the following simple chant and have him or her clap on each syllable as you say the chant: "Word, word, I know a word. How many syllables has my word?" Then suggest a word, and invite the child to guess how many syllables by clapping them out while saying the word. Then repeat the chant together again. This time invite the child to suggest a word for you to clap out in syllables.

# ECHO ME, ECHO ME — 292

*In this easy, listening exercise, the child will be your echo and repeat everything you say.*

Begin by asking the child to be your echo—that is, repeat everything you say. Start out by saying two or three words at a time for the child to echo. Then move up to sentences, first short sentences and then long sentences. Try experimenting with nonsense sounds and invite the child to try to repeat those sounds. Then trade roles and invite the child to make up words, sentences, and sounds for you to echo!

# STORY OPPOSITES

**293**

*Invite the child to demonstrate good listening skills by turning a story into its opposite.*

Take turns creating opposite versions of the same story. Begin by telling a simple story and invite the child to retell the story, changing as many things as possible to their opposites. You may want to offer suggestions to get the child started. In the story "Cinderella," for example, you might tell of how the shoe did *not* fit. After the child has taken a turn, discuss any other opposites that could be added to the story. Then invite the child to make up or read a story for you to change, or give the child another attempt at a new story.

# LITTLE, LIDDLE, LODDLE

**294**

*Changing one word a little at a time is a fun way to learn how to analyze the parts and sounds of words.*

Explain to the child that you will both take turns changing a word, one sound at a time. Then choose a word that has two or more syllables. Take the first turn and change one sound. Then invite the child to try and change another sound in the word. Continue to change the word, sound by sound, until you are both satisfied that the word is quite different than the original. Use the following example to get you started.

EXAMPLE: bubble, rubble, ripple, triple, triplet, tripping, sipping, skipping, skipper

# WHERE DID I GO?

▼▼▼▼▼▼▼▼▼▼▼▼▼▼▼▼▼▼▼▼▼▼▼▼▼▼▼▼▼▼▼▼▼▼▼▼

*This simple guessing game will stimulate the child's thinking skills while learning about interesting places.*

Begin by describing a place you have visited and the things you did there without naming the place. Then invite the child to guess where you have been. If the child is unable to guess, give him or her more clues. Continue until the child guesses correctly or until you have given ten clues.

After finishing, invite the child to describe a place that he or she has visited and see if you can guess where it is, using the same technique.

# 296 ACCUMULATING NONSENSE

*Composing with nonsense sounds is an entertaining way to blend sounds and syllables.*

Begin by creating a nonsense verse, and then invite the child to repeat that verse and add another. Continue to repeat and add new verses. Encourage the child to have fun with sounds when creating new verses. Use voice and rhythm when repeating the verses for dramatization and to help give "meaning" and impact to nonsense words!

*Oshmygosh, whooshislosh.*

*Singamodo. Callamahoo.*

*InterOffer Affer Uffer*

*Falatala Sis Matalaloo.*

Nonsense verses can rhyme or not. How much nonsense can you remember?

# TONGUE TWISTERS 297

*While saying these terribly twisted tongue twisters, you may have to un-tongue your tangle!*

Invite the child to participate in some tongue-twisting fun by saying the following tongue twisters. Encourage the child to repeat the tongue twisters faster each time.

1. Rubber baby-buggy bumper.
2. Three tall treetops.
3. How much wood would a woodchuck chuck if a woodchuck could chuck wood?
4. He shells and she sells seashells by the shady seashore.
5. Charlie Shu chooses Sherry Chu's shoes to chew.

# GRANDMOTHER'S SUITCASE

**298**

*Exercise those memory muscles with this cumulative list story!*

Start this cumulative list story by saying, "Grandmother is coming to visit. In her suitcase she will pack her pajamas." Explain to the child that he or she is to repeat everything you say and add one more item for Grandmother's suitcase. For example, the child may say, "Grandmother is coming to visit. In her suitcase she will pack her pajamas and a toothbrush."

Take another turn, and then invite the child to take another turn. Continue to repeat the original verse as well as each additional item Grandmother packs up to bring for a visit. How long of a list can be remembered?

# ALLITERATIVE ANECDOTES

**299**

*Creating alliterative anecdotes enhances skills of working with initial sounds.*

Make up and recite the beginning of a sentence in which almost all the words start with the same letter. Then invite the child to make up the end of the sentence, continuing to use words starting with that same letter. For example, you might start a sentence, "Seven silly sailors sang," and the child might end it with, "seven salamander songs."

Start again with another new sentence. This time invite the child to start the new sentence with a new letter. Try to work through the entire alphabet. Be ready for some adventurous tongue-twisting.

## ACTIVITY TWIST

For a real challenge, create a short story with the first sentence by adding more sentences that start with the same letter. You may even want to try creating a story using all the sentences that start with different letters.

# SOUND OFF

300

*Expect to hear some crazy "sounds" while reading this sound-off story!*

Read the following story with the child. Explain that while you are reading, you will be reading some words that are in capital letters. After you read the word in capital letters, the child has to make a noise that corresponds to the word. You might suggest the child use his or her voice to make noises, clap hands, tap feet, or whatever sound he or she can think of. For example, you might say, "We saw a big DOG." The child should then bark like a dog—or howl, or pant, or make whatever dog noise he or she can think of. Remind the child to make a different sound effect for each word in capital letters.

Lucky was a tabby CAT who lived in an old barn with a HORSE, a COW, a DONKEY, a ROOSTER, and an old DOG. One day Lucky the CAT was WALKING outside the barn when he saw two MICE. Lucky was a very curious CAT. When he saw that the MICE were TALKING, he tiptoed up behind them to listen.

"We have to get rid of the CAT," said the first MOUSE. "He never lets us have any fun."

"You're right," said the second MOUSE. "That CAT won't let us SING. He won't let us talk on the PHONE. He won't let us RUN. He won't let us SWIM, which is what MICE like to do best!"

"Tonight we'll have a meeting in the barn when everyone else is ASLEEP," said the first MOUSE. "We'll decide what to do with that CAT once and for all! Tell all the MICE to meet in the DONKEY'S stall at midnight."

That night, as the OWL hooted in the tree, Lucky the CAT hid behind the COW to spy on the MICE. He waited and waited, but the mice never showed up. A CRICKET on the wall said, "Look out behind you!"

Lucky the CAT turned around and saw hundreds of MICE all lined up behind him. Some of the MICE carried TRUMPETS. Some carried RATTLES. Some carried FIRECRACKERS. Some carried BELLS. And all of them were singing, "HAPPY BIRTHDAY" to Lucky the CAT.

Lucky was so happy that he whooped with delight. "That's what I get for being too curious."

# ANTONYM ANTS

**301**

*Pretend you're on a picnic, eating words. But you'll have to pick the ants out of your sentence first.*

Explain to the child that *antonyms* are pairs of words that mean the opposite of each other, such as *hot* and *cold, day* and *night, big* and *small.* The object of this activity is for the child to pick the *ant* (antonym) out of a sentence and give its opposite back to you.

For example, you say a sentence that has an antonym in it, such as "The soup is *hot.*" Explain that the antonym the child has to work into a sentence is the opposite of *hot.* The child then takes the antonym of *hot* and works it into the sentence, such as, "The water in the pool is *cold.*" The following examples will help get you started.

The soup is *hot.* (Antonym is *cold*)

The river is *deep.* (Antonym is *shallow*)

The hallway is *long.* (Antonym is *short*)

**302**

# COFFEEPOT

*In this activity, the child will coffeepot the word you're thinking of.*

Begin by thinking of a *verb* (an action word) such as *walk.* Then think of a sentence using that word. For example, "The tiger *walks* in the jungle." Next say the sentence aloud to the child, but replace the chosen verb with the word *coffeepot.* The sentence now becomes, "The tiger *coffeepots* in the jungle."

Invite the child to guess your word. If the child is unable to guess, think of a new sentence. "I *walk* to school every day," for example, would be "I *coffeepot* to school every day." Keep making up new sentences until the child guesses the word.

# TRUE OR FALSE

*Discriminating between truth and untruth can be a fun way to develop and practice reasoning skills.*

Tell the child that you are going to make five statements, four true ones and one false one. Invite the child to listen carefully to all five statements and guess which one is false. The statements can be very simple—cats like milk, the window is open, ducks have feathers, elephants swim in the ocean, we will have potato soup for lunch—or they can be more difficult—horses are mammals, the moon is a planet, bread is made from wheat, the neighbor's dog's name is Rusty, I made my bed this morning.

After doing this activity several times, invite the child to make up five statements, four true ones and one false one, and try to stump you!

# BACK-TO-BACK PICTURES

**304**

*This exercise helps the child learn to interpret verbal information through drawings.*

**WHAT YOU'LL NEED:** paper, crayons

Set up a seating arrangement in which you and the child can both draw a picture of a common object without being able to see each other's paper. The purpose of this is for the child to draw the same picture as you without looking at your drawing. Explain that you will say what you are drawing as you draw it so that the child can listen and draw the same thing. When you are finished compare drawings.

**305**

# SNAP! TAP! HEAR THAT?

*The child will develop sequencing skills essential to reading comprehension while creating sound patterns .*

Invite the child to use his or her body to create a sound pattern. The sound may include clapping, slapping your knees, snapping your fingers, or stamping your feet. Start off by demonstrating a simple pattern for the child with only three or four elements such as clap-clap-stomp, clap-clap-stomp, or snap-clap-snap-stomp, snap-clap-snap-stomp. Ask the child to listen to the pattern and repeat it. If the child has any difficulty remembering the whole pattern, repeat it again. Then invite the child to invent a pattern for you to follow. Make the patterns progressively longer as you continue to play the game.

# SPEAKING SPARKS

Writers use language to communicate meaning. Readers, in turn, use language to discern meaning. The more experiences the child has with language in all its myriad forms, the more success he or she is likely to experience at the pleasurable task of reading. Language is an active process, all of which is learned through use. The child will learn and internalize vocabulary, sentence structure, and meaning through the use of words, sentences, and sounds, all of which express ideas and emotions. Here is a wide variety of language activities to enjoy with the child that provide different ways to experiment with and experience speaking.

## 306 · STORY FLIPS

*These story-building squares offer the child infinite imaginative narrative possibilities.*

**WHAT YOU'LL NEED:** paper, 8×10-inch cardboard squares, crayons or markers, old magazines, blunt scissors, clear tape or glue

Build stories by flipping pictures the child has drawn or cut out of old magazines. The pictures should include animals, people, and objects. Help the child glue or tape each picture onto its own cardboard square. Once you and the child have assembled 12 to 20 pictures, ask the child to sort them into four random piles. Invite the child to turn over a square from each pile and then make up a story based on the four pictures. Continue with another set of four pictures for endless creative story-building fun!

The woman went shopping to buy a dog to give to her cat.

# SAME SENTENCE STARTERS

**307**

*How many sentences can the child write that start with the same word?*

Begin by choosing a word. Then invite the child to make up as many different sentences as possible that all start with the chosen word. By thinking of many possibilities, the child will be developing the skill of fluent thinking.

For example, if the word chosen is *dogs,* the child may suggest the following sentences:

Dogs like to run.

Dogs like to bark.

Dogs are the favorite animals in this family.

Dogs have fur and tails.

Dogs are sometimes walked on leashes.

**308**

# MAGAZINE PICTURE PUPPETS

*These simple puppets offer an easy way to engage the child in language expression and development.*

**WHAT YOU'LL NEED:** old magazines, cardboard, craft sticks, glue, blunt scissors

Begin by helping the child cut out pictures of people and animals from old magazines. The pictures can then be glued to cardboard for backing. Next glue a craft stick to the back of the cardboard picture to be used as a handle. When the glue on the picture puppets is dry, the child can use them to act out and tell made-up stories.

# THIRD PERSON TALES

**309**

*This activity stretches the child's ability to relay experiences from a new perspective.*

Invite the child to tell you about an event in his or her day. Explain that you want the child to tell it to you in the third person—in other words, the child should tell about an event that happened during the day as if it happened to someone else.

For example, instead of the child saying "I got up early today," the child would begin by saying "He (or she) got up early today."

**310** # NEWS REPORT INTERVIEWS

*Get the "scoop" while practicing research and organizational skills.*

**WHAT YOU'LL NEED:** paper, pencil

Invite the child to be a news reporter and report on an event that happened at home or while on a family outing. Choose a topic together for the interview. It may be something as ordinary as dinner last night or a little more unusual, such as what happened when the dog got out. Encourage the child to ask you questions that will uncover as many details as possible, then he or she should write down the answers on a piece of paper. Then invite the child to give a news report as if reporting the story on the evening news.

# FELT BOARD BACKDROPS

### 311

*The child's sequencing skills will be enhanced through this creative storytelling activity.*

**WHAT YOU'LL NEED:** cardboard, felt, old magazine pictures, blunt scissors, clear tape or glue, sandpaper

Help the child make a felt board by gluing or taping a large piece of felt or felt squares onto the cardboard. Invite the child to draw or cut out pictures of people and animals from old magazines. Then tape or glue the pictures onto small pieces of cardboard to make them sturdy. Glue a small piece of sandpaper to the back of the cardboard so the story piece will stick to the felt board. Place the pictures on the felt board, and invite the child to use the characters to dramatize and tell a made-up story or retell a favorite one.

### 312

# REARRANGED RETELLINGS

*Here is a wacky way for the child to communicate information in sequence.*

**WHAT YOU'LL NEED:** paper, markers or crayons

Help the child draw four or five separate pictures depicting four or five major events of a traditional or favorite story. Then have the child lay out the pictures in sequential order and tell the story. Then randomly rearrange the pictures and challenge the child to make up and tell a new version of the story in which the events occur in the order pictured. Expect some hilarious results!

## 313 OPPOSITE STORYTELLING

▼▼▼▼▼▼▼▼▼▼▼▼▼▼▼▼▼▼▼▼▼▼▼▼▼▼▼▼▼▼▼

*This activity will enhance the child's understanding of how speech tone and inflection can affect meaning.*

Have the child choose a favorite story and retell it using a different voice—one that does not match the tone of the story. For example, if it is a sad story, the child may tell it in a happy voice. If it is a serious story, the child may tell it in a silly voice.

## WHERE IS IT? 314

*This hide-and-describe game allows the child to practice using descriptive verbal clues.*

**WHAT YOU'LL NEED:** 2 household objects small enough to hide

Choose two small objects together. Begin by hiding one of the small objects while the child has his or her eyes closed or has gone into another room. Once the object is hidden, give the child verbal clues that describe where the object can be found without actually revealing its exact whereabouts. Once the object has been found by the child, it is your turn to close your eyes or leave the room. This time the child will hide the second object and give you verbal clues that describe where the object can be found, without revealing its exact whereabouts.

# PICTURESQUE PATTERN

*This activity helps the child develop the colorful language necessary for clear commentary.*

Begin by making a simple observation, such as "There's a bird in the tree." Then invite the child to add a descriptive word to give more information. For example, the child might say, "There's a small bird in the tree." Then you might say "There's a small bird in the large tree," and so on. Take turns and continue adding more and more descriptive words to the original statement, giving the sentence as much vivid meaning as possible.

## ACTIVITY TWIST

To extend this activity, help the child create an imaginative short story by adding more descriptive sentences.

# 316 MY NAME IS ADAM

*Here's a challenging game that encourages fast thinking and learning the alphabet.*

This alphabet chant game requires the child to think of a name, a place, and an object that begin with the same letter of the alphabet. Start the game at the beginning of the alphabet with the letter *A*. For example, you might begin by saying, "My name is Adam, I come from Alabama, and I like apples." Then invite the child to repeat the chant, replacing each *A* word with an appropriate word that starts with *B*. Then take another turn, moving into *C* words. See how many letters in the alphabet can be turned into chants.

Increase the difficulty of the game by setting a beat by clapping. Each time a new sentence is chanted, the child must speak on the beat without stopping to take extra time to come up with the right words.

# DON'T SAY WHAT YOU SEE!

**317**

*This picture description activity challenges the child to find the right words to convey meaning.*

**WHAT YOU'LL NEED:** 3×5 index cards, marker or blunt scissors, old magazines, clear tape or glue, shoe box

SIZE 5½

Create 15 to 20 picture cards of common animals or objects together. The cards can be simple line drawings on index cards or pictures cut from old magazines and glued or taped onto index cards. Put the cards in the shoe box.

Then invite the child to pull out a card and describe what is pictured without naming the object. Make sure the child keeps the card hidden from your view. You are now allowed five guesses to guess what is on the card. After the answer has been guessed or given, it is your turn to pick a card, describe what is pictured, and ask the child to guess its identity.

**318**

# WORD EMPHASIZING

*Change the meaning of a sentence by emphasizing a different word.*

Discuss the different ways of conveying meaning when using the same sentence. Make up a simple sentence and have the child repeat the sentence, emphasizing a different word each time. Talk about how the meaning of the sentence changed each time a different word was emphasized.

# 319 TRACKING DOWN WORDS

*Create a story from words found on a walk and provide an opportunity for verbal expression.*

**WHAT YOU'LL NEED:** pencil, paper

Take a walk outside together to track down words. Bring a pencil and paper along and search for words that are displayed in easy view, such as on a street sign or billboard. Write down 10 to 20 of the words discovered. When you return, encourage the child to make up a story or narration using the words that were collected. This activity also enhances the child's observation and imagination skills.

## ACTIVITY TWIST

As a variation, invite the child to walk through the house and search for 10 to 20 words to be used to create another story or narration.

# 320 **PASS-ALONG STORY**

▼▼▼▼▼▼▼▼▼▼▼▼▼▼▼▼▼▼▼▼▼▼▼▼▼

*This evolving tale-telling activity encourages fanciful thinking and comprehension.*

Create a pass-along story with the child. Choose an object to be the "pass-along" and to represent the story that gets passed along from person to person. The "pass-along" can be a stone, a stuffed animal, or a potato. You may even want to start the story about the object that is being passed along.

For example, let's say you choose a potato as the object you want to pass along. Then you would think of a story idea that would include the potato or even be about the potato. You might begin, "Once upon a time a farmer dug up a magic potato and the potato started to talk." After telling only a little bit of information, "pass along" the object (in this case the potato) to the child. Now it's up to the child to make up the next part of the story. Continue until you're both satisfied with an ending.

# **STORY STAND-UPS** 321

● ● ● ● ● ● ● ● ● ● ● ● ● ● ● ● ● ● ● ● ● ● ● ● ●

*Creating story stand-ups is a wonderful opportunity for the child to construct and convey meaning through language.*

**WHAT YOU'LL NEED:** large blank index cards or construction paper, crayons or markers

Invite the child to make stand-up drawings of characters from a favorite story for easy dramatization and retelling. First have the child fold index cards in half. Then draw the characters on one outside half of the cards, one character per card. Each character will now be able to stand up. Invite the child to use the stand-up characters to dramatize character interaction while narrating the story.

# 322 REVAMPING OLDIES

*The child can revamp a favorite song by creating new words to sing in place of the existing verses.*

This is an opportunity for the child to reinterpret a favorite song and compose new verses for it. For example, the child may want to change the words for "Mary Had a Little Lamb," to "Sally had a little bear, little bear, little bear. Sally had a little bear, and it was brown as mud." "Twinkle, Twinkle, Little Star" may be transformed into "Wiggle, wiggle, little worm. Under the ground, there you squirm."

Once the new verses have been created, invite the child to sing the newly composed version of the song.

# NEWS FLASH

**323**

*Invite the child to be a news anchor, recalling
events from a favorite story.*

**WHAT YOU'LL NEED:** pencil or pen, paper

Begin by choosing a story the child has read and is familiar with. Then help the child select and organize information, an important reading skill needed to retell a story as a newscaster. Next invite the child to report the events of the story from the point of view of a news reporter.

How would the reporter describe what happened? What would the headline be? Can the child retell the major events of the story as if it were being broadcast on the six o'clock news?

**324**

# FUNNY, FOOLISH, FALSE

*Enhance the child's understanding of the way language
can be used through this statement-making activity.*

**WHAT YOU'LL NEED:** strips of paper, pencil, small paper bag

Write words that describe different kinds of statements on strips of paper and put them into a small paper bag. Include words such as *funny, silly, false, true, exaggerated,* and *wise.* Discuss with the child the meaning of these words before you begin. Then take turns picking a piece of paper from the bag. Next make a statement that can be identified or labeled by the word written on the card. For example, if you pull out a card with the word *silly* written on it, you might say "Bears wear shoes."

# FINGER PUPPETS

● ● ● ● ● ● ● ● ● ● ● ● ● ● ● ● ● ● ● ● ● ● ● ● ●

*Make puppets from old gloves and create a cast of actors for dramatic discussion and interaction!*

**WHAT YOU'LL NEED:** old gloves or rubber dishwashing gloves, permanent markers, glue, felt or old material scraps, yarn, blunt scissors

This activity gives the child creative freedom to express thoughts and ideas through puppetry. It also provides an opportunity for the child to extend imaginative and emotional responses through language.

Begin by helping the child make faces on the fingers of clean old gloves or rubber dishwashing gloves. For rubber dishwashing gloves, draw faces with permanent markers; for cloth gloves, glue small pieces of felt, buttons, yarn, or cloth scraps for faces. Then you should carefully cut the fingers off the gloves. The child will now have finished finger puppets that can talk, sing, discuss, or whisper at the child's discretion.

# PAINT A STORY

▼ ▼ ▼ ▼ ▼ ▼ ▼ ▼ ▼ ▼ ▼ ▼ ▼ ▼ ▼ ▼ ▼ ▼ ▼ ▼ ▼ ▼ ▼ ▼ ▼

*Young artists can practice making a picture that helps tell a story.*

**WHAT YOU'LL NEED:** paper, paint, paintbrush

Invite the child to create a picture of a story. However, instead of creating an illustration for a known story, have the child draw a made-up story that you narrate. The child should illustrate each action or event as it is being told, adding more and more details to the picture and matching the telling of the story to the picture.

# PLAYFUL DEBATING

*Debating is a test of wits and knowledge and an energetic way to practice verbalizing ideas.*

Choose a topic for a playful debate with the child. You might debate about which is tastier—chocolate or vanilla ice cream? Or what's more fun—hiking or soccer?

Take turns offering reasonable arguments to support your side of the debate. You may want to have a third party listen to each of your reasons and judge which ideas and information are the strongest and most on target.

# CHARACTER TRANSPLANT 328

*Interesting situations prevail when a character is transported from its original story to new surroundings.*

Choose a character from a favorite story together. Discuss what the character is like and how it acts, reacts, solves problems, and so on. Then create a whole new story or situation and put that character in it. Invite the child to talk about what the character would do and how the character would react in that entirely new setting.

# 329 NEW ENDINGS #2

*Practice problem-solving skills while creating new endings for old stories.*

Provide examples of how stories can have many different outcomes and endings. Then invite the child to retell a favorite story or folktale as accurately as possible, with one exception: The child must make up a different ending.

# PROVE IT!

**330**

*Challenge the child to use critical thinking skills to "show what you know."*

Make a statement and ask the child to think about the statement and then guess whether the statement is true or false. After the child has answered, ask why the answer was chosen. How did the child decide or know that your statement was true or false? How can the child prove that the statement was either true or false? Encourage the child to back up his or her statement.

**331**

# MAKE IT MODERN

*In this creative retelling activity, the child brings favorite characters to life in modern times.*

Invite the child to retell a familiar folk or fairy tale, such as "The Three Little Pigs" or "Cinderella," but change the setting to modern times and to the place where you live. If the story took place today, for example, what would be the same? What would be different? If the three little pigs were building their house next door, what materials would they use? Who would they ask for supplies? If Cinderella lived in your town, where would she live? Where would the prince live? What would she wear to the ball?

# CHARACTER INTERVIEW

## 332

*Encourage the child to interpret information and make predictions while pretending to be a favorite character.*

Invite the child to pretend to be a favorite character from a favorite story. Explain that you are going to interview the character and the child should answer all your questions as the character would. Ask questions that wouldn't necessarily be found in the original story. For example, ask the character about favorite foods, what kind of stories the character likes to read, what the character wants to be when it grows up.

After you interview the child/character, choose another character together and switch roles. Now it's the child's turn to interview you!

## 333

# ELABORATE, EXAGGERATE

*The child will delight in this exaggeration game that cultivates descriptive language skills.*

Begin by making a simple statement and invite the child to add some exaggerations to it. Explain that when one exaggerates, a lot of descriptive language, real or unreal, is added. For example, if you say "The bear went to the store," the child might reply "The big bear went to the honey store." After the child adds some descriptive words, take a turn yourself and exaggerate the statement further. Continue taking turns until the original statement has become an elaborate, descriptive sentence that can be either funny or serious.

# TRADE PLACES

**334**

*You be me and I'll be you! Trade places with the child for 15 minutes of interesting conversation.*

This challenging activity is an intriguing way to practice critical thinking and interpretive skills. Pretend that you are the child and invite the child to pretend to be you. When you speak, say the things you think the child might say and use the expressions the child would use. Encourage the child to express words and ideas as you would. Then choose a topic together and have a conversation.

# SENTENCE SPROUTS

**335**

*Sentences are one of the fastest growing things on this planet. You'll see why in this activity.*

**WHAT YOU'LL NEED:** paper, pencil

Begin by saying a short phrase, such as "once upon a time" or "I know a person (or animal) named." Then have the child write down the phrase and add the necessary words to complete the sentence. When the sentence is completed, offer another phrase. Continue the activity until both of you are satisfied with the ending.

# WORD BY WORD

**336**

*Roll the dice and see who reads the next part of the story!*

**WHAT YOU'LL NEED:** dice, short story

Take turns reading aloud a short story with the child, one sentence at a time. A roll of the dice determines how many sentences each player can read per turn. Begin by rolling the dice to see who goes first. The first player then rolls the dice to determine how many sentences he or she will be able to read. The next player rolls the dice and reads the amount of sentences that are shown on the dice, starting where the last player left off. This technique helps with vocabulary building, word recall, and patience!

**337**

# LIGHTS, CAMERA, ACTION!

*While taking part in dramatizing a favorite story, the child will focus upon story comprehension.*

**WHAT YOU'LL NEED:** hats, masks, costume props

Begin by choosing a favorite story together that has lots of action. Then act it out together, or invite the child to play all the parts in the story. Use hats, masks, or simple costume props such as scarves and oversize shirts to depict the different characters.

# 338 I'M IN CHARACTER

*Stepping into character is fun and it enhances the child's ability to understand a different point of view.*

Invite the child to choose a character from a favorite story. Then have the child perform some daily activities, acting and reacting as the character would. The child might try to act in character as you prepare a meal, when cleaning up his or her room, or even while eating lunch. Encourage the child to think about how the character would react to a certain situation, and then speak or act it out based on the situation.

# SHARED WORD STORIES

### 339

*Combine groups of words chosen separately to spur story narration. Expect some creative results.*

**WHAT YOU'LL NEED:** pencil, paper

Begin by writing five words on a sheet of paper. Invite the child to do the same. Then, by sharing the words from both the child's list and your list, take turns making up and reciting a short story that includes all ten words.

### 340

# INSTANT SPEECH

*Speaking on the spur of the moment is a great way to develop organizational and expressive skills.*

**WHAT YOU'LL NEED:** watch or timer

Begin by choosing common topics together, such as dogs, trees, or the weather. Then take turns challenging one another to do a speech about what they know of the topic for one minute. As the child gains more knowledge about a topic, change the time to two minutes.

**341**

# AS THE STORY TURNS

*This is an enjoyable way for the child to practice summarizing information and sequencing skills.*

Retell a favorite and familiar story with the child, one event at a time. Invite the child to begin the story by retelling the first event in his or her own words. Then take your turn and tell the next event. Continue taking turns until the story is finished.

# TELL IT BACKWARD!

**342**

*Here's a twist on storytelling—start with the ending first!*

This challenging backward storytelling activity helps develop sequence understanding, comprehension, and story recall. Take turns retelling a favorite story with the child, only tell the story in reverse. You might want to have the book handy while retelling.

Begin telling at the end of the story. Then invite the child to tell the part that happened just before the ending. Take another turn and tell what happened before that. Continue taking turns until the whole story has been told, event by event, from end to beginning.

# 343 SAY A SONG

*Retelling song stories is a simple way to develop comprehension and practice paraphrasing information.*

Sing a song that has a story in it, such as "Mary Had a Little Lamb." Then encourage the child to retell the story using narrative form, but without repeating the verses as sung in the song.

# BACKWARD IT SAY 344

*Take turns trying to say a simple sentence backward! Backward sentence simple a say to trying turns take!*

John is name my.

This tricky word game is an intriguing way to develop memory and aids the ability to see the parts and whole of a sentence. You may want to have paper and pencil handy.

Begin by saying a simple three-word sentence. Then invite the child to say it backward. Then have the child say a simple sentence and you say it backward. Work up to four words and, eventually, five-word sentences. For a challenging variation, say a sentence backward and invite the child to turn it around.

# USING BRAIN POWER

Good readers are problem solvers. They use critical thinking skills to process the words they read. They construct meaning while they read by interpreting information, making predictions, and hypothesizing. Good readers bring a sense of curiosity to what they read. They are detectives searching for significance. They reflect on the words they process and draw conclusions based on their own prior knowledge. Good readers think while they read. Problem solving is a skill, and like any skill, it takes practice. Here is an assortment of activities that challenges the child and helps develop thinking skills.

## 345 WHAT IF?

*This game fosters imaginative thinking while the child responds to "what if" situations.*

Make up an interesting "what if" situation and invite the child to act out a response. The following are some suggestions:

What if a bird flew in the window and started playing with your toys?

What if it started raining in your house?

What if you ate a hamburger that tasted like pizza?

Have the child dramatize or explain what actions might be taken *if* a particular instance occurred. How would the child react to the particular instance?

# STORY PIE

*Inspire original storytelling by incorporating common household objects.*

**WHAT YOU'LL NEED:** 5-7 random household objects such as a sock, mixing spoon, salt shaker, hat, string

Choose five to seven common household items and lay them on a table. Challenge the child to make up and tell a silly story that includes each of the items!

# AND THEN...

347

*Engaging the child in story sequels stimulates creative thinking and problem solving.*

**WHAT YOU'LL NEED:** favorite book or story, paper, crayons or markers

Invite the child to reread a favorite book or story and imagine what might occur after the story has ended. What would the characters do next? Would there be another adventure? Encourage the child to create a sequel and tell or write the next chapter.

# NUMBER RIDDLES

**348**

•••••••••••••••••••••••••••••••••

*Inventing riddles can be a humorous way for the
child to put critical thinking skills to use.*

Invite the child to make up a number riddle and try to
stump you. Begin by sharing examples of number
riddles. Then encourage the child to invent a new one.
Here are three trusty traditional number riddles:

I'M THINKING OF SOMETHING THAT HAS FOUR LEGS AND BARKS!

What has 4 legs but never walks? (A chair)

What has 4 legs and barks? (A dog)

What has 8 legs, 2 arms, 3 heads, and wings? (A man
riding a horse carrying a canary.)

**349**

# IT'S ALL IN A NAME

▼▼▼▼▼▼▼▼▼▼▼▼▼▼▼▼▼▼▼▼▼▼▼▼▼▼▼▼▼▼

*Sentences can be captivating, especially when they
involve one's own name!*

**WHAT YOU'LL NEED:** paper, pencil

Begin by having the child write his or her name on a piece of paper. Then have the child think of
one descriptive word that starts with each of the letters in his or her first name. Each word should
tell something about the child. Next have the child use the words to write a self-descriptive
sentence. For example, if the child's name is Mary, she might choose the following words:

**M**agical      **R**ed-haired

**A**mazing      **Y**oung

# 350 THE SAME & DIFFERENT

*Play this game to develop the child's ability to perceive relationships and make comparisons.*

Name any two items, and invite the child to tell one way in which the items are similar and one way in which they are different. Begin with easy comparisons, such as a cat and a dog, and increase the difficulty as you go along. Answers for easy comparisons will be more obvious while the more difficult comparisons will require some creative thinking.

For example, the child might suggest a dog and cat are similar because they both are animals; however, the child might say they are different because one meows and the other barks. For a comparison of a star and a television, the child might suggest they both glow or you can look at both of them, but one is close and other is far away.

Accept all answers that make good connections, as there are no right or wrong answers.

# REVEALING SENTENCES 351

*Exercise creative and critical thinking while using one word as an anchor to create an entire sentence.*

**WHAT YOU'LL NEED:** pencil, paper

Choose a word that represents a person, place, or thing. The word should be plural unless it is someone's name. Invite the child to make a sentence using the letters of the word to determine the first letter of each word in the sentence. The chosen word should be the first word of the sentence.

For example, if the word chosen was *cars,* the sentence could be: **C**ars **A**re **R**eally **S**uper. A sentence for *cats* might be: **C**ats **A**re **T**imid **S**ometimes. A sentence for *Jim* might be: **J**im **I**s **M**essy.

CARS ARE
REALLY SUPER

# 352 MILLIONS OF CREATURES!

*Creating a list of creatures encourages research that is guaranteed to fascinate.*

**WHAT YOU'LL NEED:** pencil, paper

There are millions of creatures in the world—insects, birds, animals, and reptiles. How many creatures can the child name? Begin by asking the child to write down or dictate the names of all the creatures that come to mind. See how many creatures the child can list.

Keep the list in an accessible place so that new animals can be added easily as the child notices or thinks of them. Encourage the child to discover "unlisted" animals while outside, watching TV, or reading.

## ACTIVITY TWIST

To learn more about creatures, take the child on a trip to the library. Spend a few hours looking at children's encyclopedias or other children's books.

# WORD SORT

*This sorting activity is a creative way of putting information in order, a skill necessary for reading.*

**WHAT YOU'LL NEED:** pencil, paper or 3×5 index cards

Begin by creating a list together of 20 to 30 words. You may choose words randomly from a storybook; the child may even want to include words he or she is particularly fond of.

Write the words on index cards or separate pieces of paper. Then invite the child to make up categories and sort the word cards into those categories. The child may sort the words by meaning, such as things that grow, things that fly, and so on.

## ACTIVITY TWIST

Invite the child to sort the words into categories such as by number of letters in a word, number of syllables in a word, and so on.

## 354 WHAT HAPPENED FIRST?

*Narrating stories backward enhances the young thinker's comprehension and memory skills.*

In this cooperative story activity, the story is told in reverse, ending at the beginning. First invite the child to make up a story. Then have the child retell it from the end to the beginning. Help the child if necessary.

## GOOD NEWS, BAD NEWS 355

*Good news, bad news stories are fun to create and often produce a lot of laughter.*

Create a good news, bad news story together. Each person takes a turn telling something good that happened followed by something bad. The next person must continue the story by adding the next good thing followed by the next bad thing.

For example, the first person might start by saying, "I found a magic stone in the park. That was good. I lost it on the way home. That was bad." The second person might then continue with, "My friend found my stone. That was good. He wouldn't give it back. That was bad."

# MEMORY MADNESS

356

*Here's a simple activity that helps sharpen the child's ability to remember details.*

Invite the child to remember as many details as possible about a recent adventure, visit, or even a walk around the block. Then ask the child questions that challenge the child's memory skills.

What did the child hear, see, taste, smell, or touch? What was the weather like? Were there birds in the sky? Was a radio playing? What song was playing? Were people standing with their feet together or apart? Which hand petted the cat? This can be an ongoing activity for you to do periodically with the child.

357

# I'M THINKING OF . . .

*Making these simple observation puzzles helps the child practice describing what he or she sees.*

Invite the child to describe a plant, animal, object, or person that can be seen in a room without mentioning its name or what it is. See if you can guess what the child is describing. After the answer has been given, describe something you see in the room and invite the child to guess. To increase the difficulty of the game, include any plant, animal, object, or person that is not in the room.

# WHAT WILL HAPPEN?

*As with all skills, making accurate predictions takes practice. Try it and see!*

**WHAT YOU'LL NEED:** paper, pencil

Before you and the child go on an errand, shopping, or out visiting, discuss what you might see and hear and what might happen. Make a list of predictions. After returning from your trip, check the list and see how many of the predictions were accurate.

## ACTIVITY TWIST

For a challenging variation, help the child make a list of predictions for an entire week. See how many predictions come true.

# HINKIE-PINKIE

**359**

*This activity challenges the child to use critical thinking, rhyming skill, and cleverness!*

A "hinkie-pinkie" is a riddle in which the answer is a two-word rhyme. If the rhyming words have one syllable, the riddle is a "hink-pink." If the words have two syllables it is a "hinkie-pinkie."

Begin by giving the child a clue as to whether the riddle is a hink-pink, or hinkie-pinkie. Here are two examples:

Hink-Pink: What is a chubby pet that meows? (fat cat)

Hinkie-Pinkie: What is a puppy that got all soaking wet in the rain? (soggy doggy)

**360** # PEEK-A-BOO PICTURES

*This observation activity will encourage the child to see "the big picture!"*

**WHAT YOU'LL NEED:** paper, old magazine, stapler, clear tape or glue, blunt scissors

Create peek-a-boo pictures by cutting a picture from an old magazine and gluing or taping it onto a sheet of paper. Do not let the child see the picture. Next cut a small circle or square in a second piece of paper. This will be the guessing page. Then take the guessing page and lay it on top of the picture. The small portion of the picture viewed through the peek-a-boo hole becomes the clue for the child to guess the identity of the bigger picture.

# 361 THAT'S NOT WHAT I SAID

▼▼▼▼▼▼▼▼▼▼▼▼▼▼▼▼▼▼▼▼▼▼▼▼▼▼▼▼▼▼▼▼

*Create sentences with different meanings while exercising comprehension skills.*

Make up a sentence, such as the example below, and say it to the child. Then invite the child to retell the sentence but give it a different meaning, perhaps by changing the animal and the way it moved under the bridge. After the child has told a different version, retell the sentence again yourself, creating a third view that is different from the first two. Then challenge the child to create yet a fourth telling that is different from the first three versions.

1) The dog ran fast under the bridge.

2) The cat walked slowly over the bridge.

3) The mouse raced around the bridge.

4) The bird perched on top of the bridge.

# 362 SEQUENCE SENTENCES

*This game helps the child recognize sequence and organize information.*

**WHAT YOU'LL NEED:** paper strips, pencil or marker

Make up a short story or tell of a daily event using just eight to ten sentences. Write each sentence on an individual sentence strip. Mix up the strips. Then invite the child to read the strips and determine the correct sequence of the story and order the strips accordingly.

# WHAT'S THE TITLE? 363

*This inventive story-making game involves creative thinking, summarizing, and problem-solving skills.*

**WHAT YOU'LL NEED:** pictures from books or magazines

Begin by looking at a picture in a book or magazine together and discuss what you see. Pretend that one picture illustrates an entire story. Invite the child to tell you what he or she thinks the story might be about. Discuss possible details of the story. Then have the child invent a title that would fit the story.

# FANCIFUL LISTS

**364**

*Here is an imaginative and sometimes silly game
that fosters the ability to generate ideas.*

**WHAT YOU'LL NEED:** paper, pencil

Begin by brainstorming unusual topics together or by taking turns suggesting topics to each other. Make a list together or separately that contains items that might belong to a particular topic. The following are a few topics to begin with:

What are five things you'd want to be sure to take with you on a trip to the moon?

What are six unusual things you can think of to do with a paper bag?

What are seven things you could give to a hungry monster to eat?

# REBUS WRITING

▼▼▼▼▼▼▼▼▼▼▼▼▼▼▼▼▼▼▼▼▼▼▼▼▼▼▼▼▼▼▼

*Test the child's creative thinking, problem-solving skills, and ability to translate pictures into words.*

**WHAT YOU'LL NEED:** construction paper, felt-tip pen, markers

Begin by creating sentences for the child to translate by representing some of the words with pictures. As you write the sentence, draw certain words, especially repeated words, as pictures. For example, if you wrote a sentence about a king, you could draw a picture of a crown as the symbol for the word *king.* Then challenge the child to translate rebus sentences you have created. The following are two examples to get you started.

# Index